FORTUN[illegible]

A unique modern ma[illegible] divination by dice – a development of the ancient practice of casting lots.

In this series:

FORTUNE-TELLING BY PLAYING CARDS
Nerys Dee

FORTUNE-TELLING WITH TAROT CARDS
Stuart R. Kaplan

FORTUNE-TELLING BY DICE

Uncovering the Future Through the Ancient System of Casting Lots

by

DAVID AND JULIA LINE

PARRAGON

This edition published 1997 by Diamond Books for

Parragon
Units 13–17, Avonbridge Industrial Estate
Atlantic Road, Avonmouth
Bristol BS11 9QD

First published in the UK by the Aquarian Press 1984
Reprinted 1985

ISBN 0 752 51948 4

Printed in Great Britain by
Caledonian International Book Manufacturing Ltd, Glasgow

CONTENTS

	Page
Introduction	9
Chapter	
1. A History of Dice	11
2. Dice and Games	15
3. The Symbols of the Red Dice	19
4. The Symbols of the White Dice	33
5. The Symbols of the Green Dice	47
6. How to Cast	59
7. Sample Casts	65
8. Interpretations	73
Bibliography	155
Index	157

To G.H.L. and C.E.L., without whom the authors still would not have been possible.

INTRODUCTION

Looking back on past events in our lives most of us, at one time or another, have said 'I wish I had done so and so differently' or 'Why didn't I choose to do something else?' In even the most mundane life, the choices which face each individual during the course of one day are enormous. And, each action, taken as the result of what we like to think is free choice, can turn out to be the first step towards disaster or success. 'If only I'd stayed another ten seconds talking to that man, I wouldn't have arrived at the very moment three cars collided . . . and mine was one of them.'

The key words are 'if only' but they are, by nature, retrospective. And there's no value in looking back at what might have been. The English language is full of adages to suit that attitude of mind . . . 'it's no good closing the stable door after the horse has bolted' . . . 'you've made your bed, now you must lie on it' . . . and, most appropriate to this book . . . 'the die has been cast'.

There is, of course, value in looking back and learning from our mistakes. But then how many people can honestly say they do that! What has intrigued mankind more, is the possibility of looking forward. Not necessarily to determine each and every action to be taken throughout life, but to get some overall indication of trends and patterns, good and bad. At the most basic level, fortune-telling is synonymous with intuition. It's intuition that tells us not to do something, or that someone will be good or bad for us. It's thought-based, not on logic or just sensation but, if you like, on the vestiges of some sixth sense.

It is not coincidental that intuition also plays a major part in most forms of fortune-telling and divination. It is intuition which puts the meat on the divinatory bones of tarot, runes or I Ching readings. Add to this palmistry, astrology, numerology and the almost countless other disciplines, and we can see that it is 'perception through intuition' which is the common denominator.

It is equally no coincidence that many, of what we take to be simple games of chance, have their origins not in the development of pastimes and leisure interests, but in divination and fortune-telling. In this way the nature of such words as 'chance', 'luck' and 'fortune' and 'fortune-telling' have become inextricably mixed.

Perhaps the most dramatic game of chance is dice. Unlike games involving cards or even roulette (the wheel of fortune?), dice is fast, active and very simple. As far as we can tell, it is probably the oldest game of chance known to man, it is probably also the oldest method used for telling fortunes. But, like all the other methods of divination, dice are only the tools of the trade. They are not intrinsically capable of telling fortunes, neither can any mystic or occult powers be attributed to them. The accuracy of divination using dice is only as good as the reader can make it. The dice provide the keys for the diviner to unlock the querent's future.

1
A HISTORY OF DICE

'Fair in our lot – O goodly is our heritage!'
A Song of the English – Kipling

Casting dice, lots or bones for both gaming and divination is almost as old as mankind itself. Primitive man invented divinatory games in order that the gods could give signs for the future to those able to interpret the symbols.

In ancient Egypt, during the Archaic Period, throwsticks were tossed into the air by individuals faced with problems in need of solution and the outcome of the throw would decide which course of action they would take. Throwsticks, the forerunners of dice, were simply tubular wands between three to nine inches long made from split reeds and usually they came in sets of four, five or six and sometimes more. Examples have been found made from wood and ivory. One face was slightly concave and left undecorated, the other was convex and carved or engraved. When thrown, they fell randomly either face up or face down. They bear some resemblance to the yarrow sticks in I Ching, although the way they are used is different.

Primitive people throughout the world, among them Africans, Eskimos and Mayans, have employed dice of various shapes and markings and of many different materials – horn, teeth, peach stones and pottery. During Greek and Roman times many were made from ivory, crystal, amber and porcelain. However, the original 'lots' were made from the astragali or knuckle bones of animals such as goats and sheep.

The astragal is a small, uneven, four-sided bone found within the tarsal joint of most hooved animals. The curved sides were filed flat and each face inscribed with mystic symbols. The Greeks, however, preferred to leave their knuckle bones intact as each of the four long faces is different – one convex, another concave, the third nearly flat and the fourth sinuous and irregular. They chose not to mark their astragali since their sides were easy to distinguish. Some Greek dice are particularly interesting because of their unusual shape – squatting figures with their knees bent and with their hands on hips, modelled in silver. They were marked with the numbers 1-6 on different parts of the body. Astragali are still used today among some Arab and Indian tribes. In fact the Arabic word for knucklebone is the same as that for dice.

In Roman mythology Mercury was the patron of dice-players and was most frequently depicted standing on tiptoe with his heels clear of the ground. His winged sandals were called talaria, from the word talus which means heel. And from the same root word, the Romans called their dice tali because they came from the heel bones of sheep and goats – the sacred animals of Mercury. Mercury used dice to foretell the future and, in honour of his mother, he used a set of five four-sided marked dice. However, in ancient times, three six-sided dice were also deemed to make a set.

There are a number of references in the Bible to 'casting lots' which indicate that astragali were not only used for games but also for sharing property and ending arguments – but essentially for divination. St Thomas points out that 'there is no harm in casting lots to decide a dispute provided that no knowledge is attributed to the objects themselves and that no appeal is made to the Evil One!' He also says that 'If there is need, it is lawful with all due reverence to seek judgement of God by lots.' And Proverbs 16:33 contends that though the lot is thrown, 'the decision is wholly from the Lord.' Lots were cast to choose the first King of Israel (I Samuel 10:20-21) and also to decide upon the distribution of the crucified Jesus' clothes between the soldiers who were present at the time (St John 19:23-24).

Astragali have been discovered in large numbers in many excavations of prehistoric sites and, perhaps as long ago as 40,000 years, people were casting these bones in games of chance – unfortunately the rules and methods of play are not fully known today. Archaeologists have found artefacts used in Egyptian games of chance dating from as early as 3500 BC as well as tomb paintings and drawings on pottery illustrating people or gods tossing astragali and using counting boards to keep score of the game. In the Egyptian Gallery of the British Museum there is a fine example of an ivory astragal which belonged to Queen Hatesu circa 1600 BC.

The earliest known dice from Iraq and India date from about 3000 BC. The Aryan invaders of India in the second millenium BC loved to gamble and dice games with vibhidata nuts were popular among most people except the very religious. It is in India more than 2000 years ago that the first written records of dice are found in the ancient Sanskrit epic, the *Mahābhārata*. The *Rgveda*, a collection of Vedic hymns includes a poem entitled the 'Gamester's Lament' one verse of which quotes the god Savitr:

> Don't play with dice but plow your furrow!
> Delight in your property, prize it highly!
> Look to your cattle and look to your wife, you gambler!
> Thus noble Savitr tells me.

Sophocles and Herodotus have both made claims regarding the invention of dice – and both of their claims have been discredited by numerous archaeological finds of earlier dates. Sophocles stated that dice were invented by Palamedes, a Greek, during the siege of Troy about 1244BC while Herodotus believed that the Lydians invented them, along with balls and other playthings, during a time of famine in the days of King Atys when they would play and eat on alternate days. However, it is known that Palamedes did in fact invent Draughts at the time of the Trojan War and perhaps this is where the confusion arose.

Gambling with dice was a popular pastime among the ancient Greeks and Romans. Dicing was actually declared illegal during the later days of the Roman Empire and was only officially permitted during the annual Saturnalia feasts. This law, however, was generally ignored and many famous Romans were on familiar terms with dice. Nero and Augustus were both keen dice players, Mark Anthony played dice during his stay in Alexandria and Caligula was a notorious cheat. The Emperor Claudius went one step further and actually penned a book on dice games.

Around 1400 BC the arrangement of the points which we still use today was developed. The spots were arranged in conventional patterns and placed so that the spots on the opposite side always total seven – 1+6, 2+5 and 3+4. The early German tribes were known to gamble for both people and property with dice (as described by Tacitus) and occasionally even tribal battles were concluded with a game of chance.

From AD 960 onwards when Wibold wrote about his clerical dice game with its fifty-six 'Virtues' (the number of ways three dice can be thrown irrespective of order which the player was supposed to practice) there have followed many other learned papers on the subject of dice. During the 13th century Richard de Fournival, a Frenchman and a humanist, is believed to be the author of a poem written in Latin which includes a stanza setting out the first known calculation of the 216 separate ways of throwing three dice.

In the year AD 1526 the first mathematical analysis of the cast of the dice was written by Gerolamo Cardano the Italian physician, mathematician and astrologer. With a personal theoretical argument he attempted to set down the relative probabilities of the separate combinations, the idea of purely random activity and its relationship between chance and probability. Cardano numbered among his accomplishments considerable first hand experience of games of chance and gave advice on laying wagers to his students.

The science of probability has its roots in the everyday problems of games of chance. In the late 1500s Galileo turned his attention to the analysis of dicing at the request of disappointed gamesters who had suffered heavy losses, as did Pascal in 1654. The calculations used by Galileo are exactly the same as those that mathematicians would employ today. However, the greatest theoretical advance did not come until the 1750s when Christiaan Huygens wrote his famous treatise entitled *De Ratiociniis in Lundo Aleae* (On Ratiocination in Dice Games).

Dicing was a popular and fashionable pastime both in this country and on the continent from the Middle Ages right up until the 19th century, although from the 17th century onwards it saw a steady decline as both card games and horse-racing increased in popularity.

One final point of historical interest concerning dice takes us back to 1711 when the British Government imposed a duty on dice. In 1804 the duty stood at £1 which was an exorbitant sum. The dice had to be wrapped in official Government paper and sealed with wax. This duty was finally abolished in 1850.

2
DICE AND GAMES

Dice are essential to many of the games children and adults play such as Monopoly, Snakes and Ladders, Ludo and so on. Yet the combination of a board game and dice goes back into our earliest history. It is likely that seers, sages and soothsayers would have used highly decorated boards and dice as part of their mystical equipment. And the symbolism which all these components contained would have been geared to the needs of those illiterate people who consulted the wise ones.

A picture says a thousand words – an adage which is much used in today's world of publishing – and the pictures and symbols which would have decorated these boards said far more than a meaningless jumble of words. It is probable that the picture images used in Tarot – the Devil's picturebook – developed in much the same way. With improvements in education and literacy, it is believed that the 'fortune-telling gameboards' developed into the harmless parlour games we know today.

Sir Leonard Woolley, the British archaeologist, discovered the oldest gaming boards known in the royal tombs of Ur. These date from about 3000 BC. No account of how the game was played exists but the players each had seven pieces and six pyramidic dice were used to make the moves. Three lapis lazuli and three white dice made up the set.

Backgammon (from the Anglo Saxon 'bac' meaning back and 'gammon' meaning game) probably appeared in England as early as the tenth century and evolved from the Egyptian 'Game of

Thirty Squares' also called 'Senet'. Many of the boards used in this game have been discovered in tombs of the Empire Age – about 1580 BC.

Greek women played a game called 'five-stones' – a name still given by children to a very similar game. The five stones were in fact five astragali and the game has been described by Pollux, the lexicographer, in this way:

> The knucklebones are thrown up into the air, and an attempt is made to catch them on the back of the hand. If you are only partially successful, you have to pick up the knucklebones which have fallen to the ground, without letting fall those already on the hand.

The Romans and Greeks had many ways of playing with dice and this example is one of the most interesting – it is also believed to have been the most popular in those days. Three dice were used and each of the players had to attempt to throw the highest number. Three sixes, which was obviously the best anyone could achieve, became proverbial. The watchman in Aeschylus' Agamemnon, when he saw the beacon fire which signalled Agamemnon's victorious homecoming, exclaimed: 'I'll count my master's fortunes fallen fair, now that my beacon watch has thrown a triple six'. With astragali 1, 3, 4, 6 was the best throw and was nicknamed 'the throw of Venus', each bone had to show a different face. The worst throw of all, called 'Dogs' occurred when four 1's turned up.

The game of 'chance bone', played by children in former times with hucklebones, bears a striking resemblance to the game of Hazard which is played with two dice. The player who throws first is called the 'caster' and his opponent the 'setter'. This game was made illegal during George II's reign when 'all games invented or to be invented with one or more die or disc' were outlawed. The reason for this ban was to attempt to stamp out the use of 'crooked dice' by unscrupulous swindlers who were always ready to cheat honest citizens. Any dice that is not a perfect cube will not act according to correct mathematical odds. Crooked dice are called 'shapes' and the most common of these have had one or more of their sides shaved down.

Another illegal dice game, which originated in the Navy and was extremely popular amongst the sailors, is Crown and Anchor.

The game is played on a square of oil-cloth which has been marked with the following symbols – a crown, an anchor and the aces of Spades, Hearts, Diamonds and Clubs. Three dice, also marked with these six symbols, are used. The player who has been elected as 'banker' throws the three dice, after the other participants have decided which of the six symbols they wish to back and, of course, handed him their stake money. According to the number of dice on which his choice appears the player wins once, twice or three times his stake. However, should his choice fail to appear – he loses his money.

Apart from being objects employed in both divination and games of chance, dice also have some interesting symbolism and beliefs connected with them. In Hinduism the die takes on the symbolism of the cube – the four square of the sacred four and the cycles of the yugas. Breaking dice in two also symbolised the making of a contract or the renewal of friendship, while in Christian beliefs it stands for the passion of Christ. In India geometric forms have cosmic implications and, in this context, the cube represents the earth. The Western mind sees the cubic dice as symbols of matter and because only three faces of a die are visible at any one time they are also symbolic of the Trinity.

From a numerical point of view it has already been mentioned that opposite faces add up to seven – 1+6, 2+5 and 3+4 – but if these three sevens are multiplied thus 7 x 7 x 7 – plus the added value of all the dots (1-6 inclusive), plus one for the die itself, you get the number 365 – the number of days in a year. The twelve edges of the dice represent the months and the four lateral sides equal the four seasons and the cardinal directions.

3

THE SYMBOLS OF THE RED DICE

RED DICE – SIX SPOTS – BAT

'For the black bat, night, has flown' – just one line from *'Maud'* by Alfred, Lord Tennyson which shows quite clearly one view of this creature – something black and usually evil, a creature of the night and darkness, transitory – of a passing nature. In medieval Europe it was linked with death and witchcraft and thought to fly with its head down because its brain is heavy. Its wings were also looked on as an infernal attribute.

In China, however, the bat was associated with happiness and long life as it supposedly lived to be a thousand. Bat talismans were worn to promote longevity. They were often made in the form of five bats linked together when they stood for luck, wealth, longevity, health and peace – 'that which all men desire'. Occasionally only two bats were depicted to symbolize good wishes. This two-bat talisman was a favourite gift between friends. To the Japanese they symbolized happiness and prosperity and were called komori.

There is a tenuous link between the bat and the Hanged Man in Tarot, as they are both symbolic of inversion – they are both objects which are depicted upside-down. The bat is symbolic of shadow. Just as the sun represents the light side of the spirit, the bat, in its role of shadow, is the negative 'double' of the body – the image of its evil and base side. Primitive people regarded shadow as the soul, or 'alter ego' – a belief which is echoed in the literature and folktales of some advanced cultures. Jung used the term 'shadow' to mean the primitive and instinctive side of an individual.

In Finno-Ugric a bat was believed to be one of the forms the soul can take during sleep, and for this reason it was not seen during the day when people are awake. In Bohemia, to carry the right eye of a bat was thought to bring invisibility.

Key Words and Phrases: a passing shadow which can hide good and evil, warning, danger signal, omen, prediction, prophecy.

Subsidiary meanings:

Passing – course of time, matter of time, process of time, lapse of time, march of time, duration, progress, flow, run, roll, proceed, advance, run its course, expire, end, go by, pass by, enjoy a spell, in due time, fullness of time, with the days, approach towards, in transit.

Shadow – dream, ghost, illusion, smokescreen, cloak, blanket, veil, cover, darken, cloud, fog, mist, glaze, make opaque, obscure, blur, overcast, vague, undefined, confused, indistinct, conceal, loom, cover.

Hide – conceal, camouflage, disguise, smoke-screen, mystify, suppress, unintelligible, mask, confine, keep in, lock up, seclude, seal up, bottle up, cover over, gloss over, stifle, smother, keep back, reserve, withhold.

Good – blessing in disguise, for the best, to one's advantage, luck, windfall, favourable, happy, prosperous.

Evil – mischieviousness, foul play, to one's cost, nuisance, annoying, harm, damage, injurious, troubles, troublesome.

Danger Signal – warning, alarm-bell, alert, omen, prediction, prophecy, forwarned, distress signal, alert, arouse, frighten, startle.

RED DICE – FIVE SPOTS – BEETLE

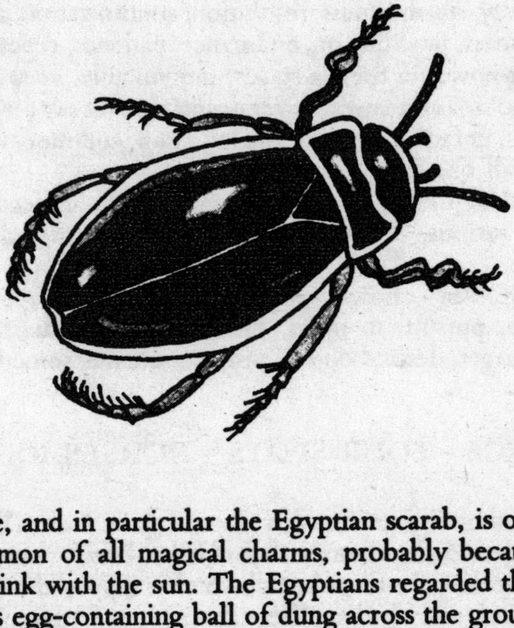

The beetle, and in particular the Egyptian scarab, is one of the most common of all magical charms, probably because of its symbolic link with the sun. The Egyptians regarded the beetle, pushing its egg-containing ball of dung across the ground, as an earthly equivalent of the sun, that great ball of light which appears to be rolled across the sky. It also symbolizes the hope of a life hereafter.

The Egyptian scarab beetle, like the crab, has as its function the attribute of devouring what is transitory – the volatile element in alchemy – and of contributing to moral and physical regeneration. It is interesting to note that scarab is the word source of both crab and scar.

The beetle is a vital component of a South American Indian legend. They believed that this creature created the world and from the grains of earth he had left over he fashioned man and woman. The Ancient Hebrews, like the Egyptians, believed that the beetle procreated as it walked backwards towards the west, the region of darkness, and it became symbolic of darkness, obscurity and shadows.

Key Words and Phrases: doggedness, determination, single-mindedness, purposefulness, specific ambition, targets.

Subsidiary meanings:

Doggedness – perseverance, persistence, tenacity, stubbornness, obstinacy, steadfastness, resolution, concentration, application, tirelessness, plodding on, endurance, patience, repeated efforts, staying power, a trier, a stayer, indomitable, keep at it, never take 'no' for an answer, never despair, never say die, have what it takes, unfailing, try, try and try again, continue, keep going, work till one drops, hang on.

Determination – fixity of purpose, compulsion, unbending, intent upon, serious, devoted, dedicated, see it through, take the plunge.

Specific Ambition – chosen, special, named, decided upon, purpose, resolve, pursuit, in mind, future intention, desire, ultimate goal, target, desired object, project, scheme, something to aim at.

RED DICE – FOUR SPOTS – HORSESHOE

The horseshoe is a universal symbol of good luck. This luck has been attributed for a number of reasons. Firstly, horseshoes are made from iron, the magic metal which is supposed to drive away witches and evil spirits. They are fashioned by blacksmiths, workers with fire and iron, who for centuries were believed to have special powers. Also, they are closely connected with the horse, a sacred beast in many cultures, symbolic of virility and fertility and ridden by heroes and gods. Finally, they resemble, in shape, the crescent moon, symbol of Isis.

Horseshoes were especially lucky if they were found on the road where a horse had cast them. The usual practice was to take the shoe home and nail it over the front door or threshold. Care

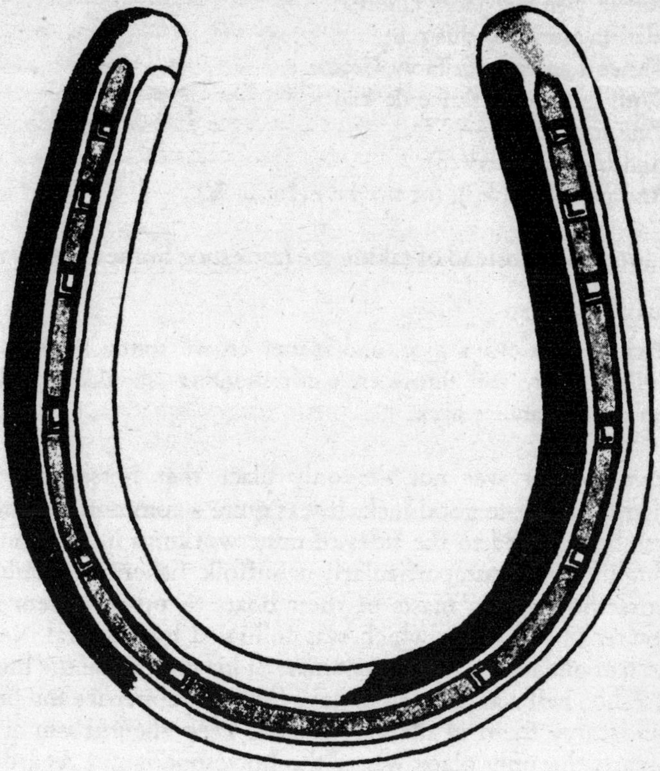

had to be taken, however, to ensure that the horseshoe was hung the correct way up. The points had to face upwards so that the good luck would not drain away. Another belief was that bad luck was trapped in the circle and because the devil cannot cross the opening he would keep running backwards and forwards inside. The luckiest horseshoes to find have four nails on one side and only three on the other which totals seven, a number which is believed to be extremely fortunate. If a young girl found a horseshoe the nails left on it were said to number the years before she would marry.

Christian and pagan beliefs often became interwoven in many old superstitions. The following charm, which should be recited aloud while nailing a horseshoe over the door, is one such example:

Father, Son and Holy Ghost,
Nail the devil to this post,
Thrice I smite with Holy Crook,
With this mell I thrice do knock,
One for God,
And one for Wod(en),
And one for Lok(i), (or maybe even 'luck').

In Shropshire, instead of taking the horseshoe home another ritual was used:

> Pick'en up'e'orse's shoe, and spatter en wi' spittle. Mak' a wish fully quickly and throw en o'er't shoother (shoulder), walk by an' ne'er glance'e back.

Above a door was not the only place that horseshoes were nailed to promote good luck. It was quite a common sight to see horseshoes nailed to the sides of mine workings in this country. Along the east coast, particularly in Suffolk, fishermen would nail a horseshoe to the masts of their boats to protect them from shipwreck, a practice which was followed by Admiral Nelson, who had one nailed to the mainmast of his ship. Even the humble horseshoe nail was deemed to have magical properties and people would carry them in their pockets to keep rheumatism at bay. China is the only place where the horseshoe is not regarded as being a source of good fortune. There, the entire hoof of a horse is looked upon as a symbol of good luck.

In the Middle Ages the combination of ash tree wood and horseshoe was an important medicinal charm. The practice was to bury a shoe in the roots of the tree. Sometimes it was hung on an ash bough so that the branches would eventually grow round it. Twigs from an ash tree, which had been treated in this fashion, were brushed over the backs of sick cattle to cure them of their ailments.

Key Words and Phrases: good fortune, happiness, laughter, good luck especially in a gamble, successful plans.

Subsidiary meanings:

Good Luck/Good Fortune – prosperity, well-being, hapiness, health and wealth, success, have all the luck, crest of the wave, affluence, plenty, luxury, golden touch, Midas touch, fat of the land, smile of fortune, blessings, luck, prestige, bed of roses, halcyon days, thriving, up and coming, fortunate, make hay, fall on one's feet, turn out well, run of luck, on a good thing.

Happiness – joy, pleasure, enjoyment, pleasant times, merry, blissful, have the pleasure, pleased, delight in, relish, have fun.

Laughter – rejoicing, thanksgiving, be joyful, celebrate, let yourself go, make merry, flash a smile, loosen up, unwind, fun and games.

Gamble – risk-taking, plunge, risk, hazard, speculate, flutter, leap in the dark, have a go, experiment, chance, venture, try your luck, risk it.

Successful – happy ending, favourable issue, time well spent, breakthrough, achieve, accomplish, triumph, win, effective, profitable, foolproof, make the grade, arrive, show results, bear fruit, do the trick.

Plans – intentions, calculations, future pursuits, projects, designs, schemes, proposals, objects, ends, have every intention, aim at, strive after, heart set upon, promise oneself, aspire to, dream of, eye upon.

RED DICE – THREE SPOTS – BOAT

A wet sheet and a flowing sea,
  A wind that follows fast
And fills the white and rustling sail
  And bends the gallant mast;
And bends the gallant mast, my boys,
  While like the eagle free
Away the good ship flies, and leaves
  Old England on the lee.

—*A. Cunningham.*

Stirring lines – and what a picture they evoke of excitement, travel and adventure with a great sailing vessel outward bound in search of new lands and new routes between distant peoples. The boat has been replaced by a boot on modern dice and, although some of the imagery has been lost, the interpretation remains the same.

Boat and ship are synonymous and in Christian symbolism the ship represents the Christian church. In the most general sense boats represent 'a vehicle' and the opportunity for travel and

discovery. Before the advent of 'air mail' letters from overseas were carried by sea and the boat has become linked with news from a distance – messages and communications.

The ship has often been described as the Solar Boat (life) making its voyage across the Ocean – a symbol of the unconscious and darkness. And the ship of death is the means by which the body is carried from one life to the next. Life, when represented as a boat, can be steered and the most profound significance of navigation is that implied by Pompey the Great when he said – 'Living is not necessary, but navigation is.'

Key Words and Phrases: travel, outward journeys, expeditions, quests, searches, movement, messages and communications.

Subsidiary meanings:

Travel – successive change of place, make journeys, movement, going, march on, motion towards, move, go, make your way, remove, change places, set going.

Outward Journeys – projection, outgoing, outward bound, departure, exodus, travel, itinerancy, globe-trotting, tourism, voyage, passage, trip, expedition, course, trek, business trip, errand, progress, tour, jaunt, joy ride, outing, excursion, wanderlust, rambling, stopping-over, visiting, nomadic, migratory, footloose, see the world, explore, go places, sightsee, go forth, take wing, wend one's way, gad about.

Quests/Searches – pursuit, enterprise, hunt, search-party, in quest of, sent after, in pursuit, in full cry, on the trail, seek, look for, cast about, follow the scent, track, be after, aim at, intend, undertaking, obligation, labour of love, adventure, probe, treasure-hunt, enquire, question, ransack, rummage, comb, go through, grope for, seek a clue.

Movement – motivation, coming and going, hive of industry, plenty to do, pressure of work, things going on, restlessness, energy, activity, bustle, eventful, hard at it.

Messages/Communications – notification, bulletin, announcement, declaration, news, report, information, tidings, word of mouth, cable, telegram, letter, postcard, telephone, signal, intelligence.

RED DICE – TWO SPOTS – SKULL

Behold this ruin! 'Twas a skull
Once of ethereal spirit full!
This narrow cell was Life's retreat;
This place was Thought's mysterious seat!
What beauteous pictures fill'd that spot,
What dreams of pleasure, long forgot!
Nor Love, nor Joy, nor Hope, nor Fear,
Has left one trace, one record here.

Lines to a skull – Anna Jane Vardill – 1816

The skull is not the most pleasant of symbols and is a constant reminder to man of his own mortality. It represents death, transitoriness and the vanity of earthly life. The skull, like a snail's shell, is what survives the living once the body has gone forever. For this reason it becomes significant as a receptacle of life and thought. Leblant describes the skull as 'the semi-spherical crown of the human body' which signifies the heavens, whilst Plato in *Timaeus* declares that 'the human head is the image of the world.'

Skulls were once objects employed in divination. The origin of the belief in a head discoursing after death probably has its roots in such legends as Arthur, Bran, Mimir and Orpheus. This idea can also be found in Shakespeare's *Hamlet*. In Norse mythology it was believed that the heavens were made from the skull of Ymir, a primaeval giant.

Key Words and Phrases: mortality, death, change by transformation, sudden unexpected change, alterations, new situations.

Subsidiary meanings:

Mortality – impermanence, brittleness, fragility, briefness, time-bound, passing, for the moment, here today gone tomorrow.

Death – extinction, destruction, abolition, end of, finish, cancellation, wipe clean, vanished, no more, obsolete, over and done with, pass away, leave no trace, cancel, abolish, wipe out.

Transformation – alteration, variation, difference, adjust, swap, improvement, convert, adapt, revise, reform, unrecognizable, change the form, appearance or character of, alter out of all recognition.

Sudden/Unexpected – unprepared, surprise, shock, jolt, bolt from the blue, bombshell, eye-opener, revelation, amazing, unguessed, unforseen, not-anticipated, unannounced, improbable, not bargained for, unaccountable, taken aback, caught napping, sprung on, bowl over, without notice.

New Situations – not previously in existence, modern, recent, unheard of, up to date, revolutionary, move with the times, circumstances, environment, look of things, lay of the land, positions, settings, locations, directions, bearings, job, station, predicament.

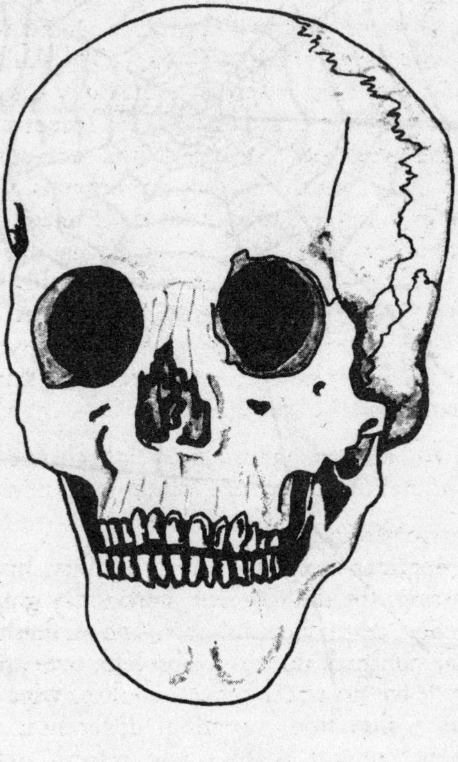

RED DICE – ONE SPOT – WEB

The web of our life is of a mingled yarn, good and ill together.

All's Well That Ends Well – Shakespeare.

As a symbol the web needs little explanation – it represents just what it is – a trap, an illusion and a source of danger to the unwary. Symbolically the web and the spider are closely linked – one is the trap, the other the trapper. The Mayans regarded the spider as the eternal weaver of the web of illusion. They also believed that death wound up the thread of an old life in order to spin a new one.

The web can be viewed not only as a symbol of life, destiny and fate but also as a spiral net converging to a central point – the centre of the world.

The last words on the subject should come from Scott. In his poem *Marmion* he sums up the whole concept in just two lines:

> O what a tangled web we weave
> When first we practice to deceive.

Key Words and Phrases: involvement, entanglement, confusion, illusion, traps, pitfalls.

Subsidiary meanings:

Involvement – confuse, complicate, perplex, involve, entangle, embroil, deception, guile, trickery, pretence, insincerity.

Illusion – misrepresentation, deception, distortion, confuse, sleight of hand, not what it seems, pretence, fraud, trickery, crafty, cunning, hoax, doublecross, take advantage of, pull the wool over one's eyes.

Traps/Pitfalls – lay a trap, entangle, net, trip up, catch out, lure, decoy, entice, tempt, waylay, lie in wait, source of danger, boobytrap, trapdoor, thin ice, powder-keg, trouble spot, hornet's nest, hidden hand, snake in the grass.

4

THE SYMBOLS OF THE WHITE DICE

WHITE DICE – SIX SPOTS – CROSSROADS

'Dirty work at the crossroads' is a well-known saying which conjures up foul play and nefarious activities. This association has probably come about because murderers and suicides (who were excluded from holy rites) were, at one time, buried at crossroads. And in the case of murderers they were sometimes hanged there too. The ancient Teutonic people used such places for holding sacrifices to their gods and by association they came to be places of execution. During the Middle Ages the crossroads was also used as a rendezvous for witches and demons.

This meeting place of roads is symbolic of a choice of direction, a chance to change direction and just simply what it is – a meeting place.

Key Words and Phrases: hidden surprises, strangers, outsiders that can cause contentions and influence the home and family, decisions.

Subsidiary meanings:

Hidden Surprises – concealed, camouflage, disguise, smokescreen, unintelligible, mask, keep back, reserve, withhold, unexpected, unprepared, sudden, shock, jolt, bolt from the blue, bombshell, revelation, amazing, unguessed, unforseen, not anticipated, unannounced, improbable, not bargained for, without notice.

Strangers/Outsiders – intruder, interloper, foreigner, person in a

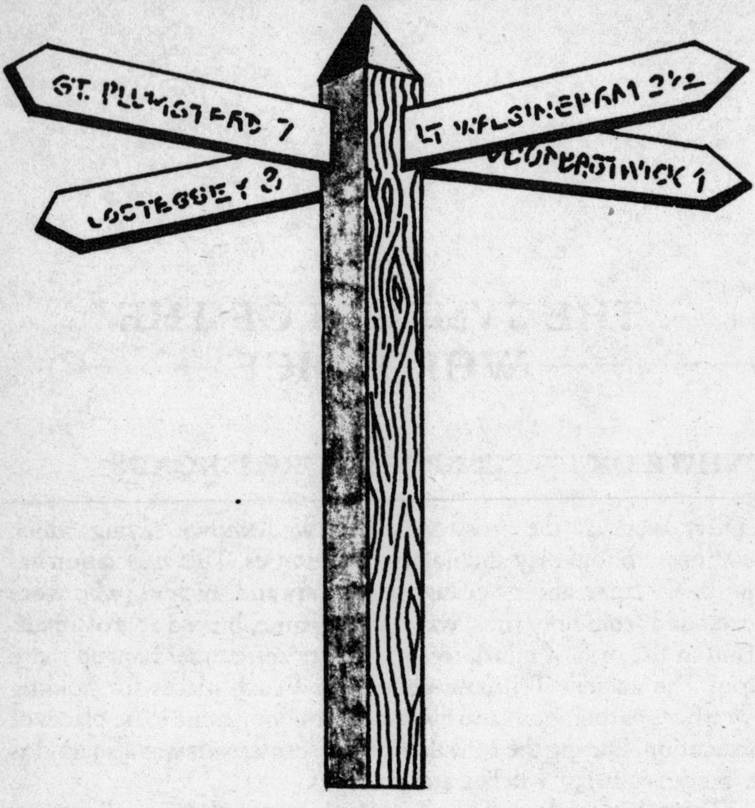

place or in company that he does not belong to, unknown, non-member of the circle or party.

Cause Contentions – create, produce, bring about, result in, breed, stir up, construct, build, form, – quarrels, disputes, clashes, conflicts, trouble, arguments, make mischief, divide, set against, areas of disagreement, jealousy, disharmony, set at odds, clashes.

Influence – jaundice, prejudice, leverage, hold, grip, pressure, cause, pull strings, dominate, work upon, induce, persuade, convince, colour, infect, have a hold on.

Decisions – reach a stage, turning point, moment, opportunity, focus, centre, reach opinion, decree, estimate, calculate, sum up.

WHITE DICE – FIVE SPOTS – CAT

Cats – sleek, cruel and stealthy – are symbols of mystery and occult powers. No self-respecting witch in the Middle Ages would have been without her feline familiar, and many an innocent villager was put to death on the suspicion of witchcraft just for owning one. In classical legend one of the priestesses of Hecate, the queen of witchcraft and sorcery, would often take on the form of a cat. To the Romans the cat was a symbol of liberty and freedom, probably because of the animal's hatred of restraint.

The colour of a cat is often very important as far as superstition and folklore are concerned. However, in America a cat, regardless of colour, seen washing its ears excessively was regarded as a flood warning. Black cats have long been associated with witchcraft and the devil but during the trial of the Chelmsford witches in 1566 a white-spotted cat named Sathan was accused of many nefarious deeds including murder. Black cats are sometimes thought of as lucky although the Chinese dislike them as they are, to them, a warning of sickness. On the island of Guernsey a stranger is expected if a black cat passes the window, and a cat with double claws is doubly lucky and should be treated with great care.

Conway in his book *Demonology and Devil Lore* states that a tri-coloured cat will protect the house in which it lives against fire. He goes on to say that a black cat protects gardens and can cure epilepsy although he doesn't say how.

Key Words and Phrases: home, marriage, the family circle, children, relatives.

Subsidiary meanings:

Home – abode, place of habitation, address, residence, domicile, hang-out, roof over one's head, lair, den, homestead, birthplace, home ground, manor, bricks and mortar, avenue, roost.

Marriage – wedlock, conjugal bliss, matrimony, wedding, nuptials, man and wife, mate, partner, husband, wife, lord and master, other half, pair, joined, couple, for better or worse.

Family Circle – relations, kindred, kith and kin, descendants, ancestors, offspring, flesh and blood, twin, brother, sister, cousin, aunt, uncle, stock, breed, strain, line, tribe, clan.

WHITE DICE – FOUR SPOTS – KNIFE

Come, thick night,
And pall thee in the dunnest smoke of hell
That my keen knife see not the wound it makes
Nor heaven peep through the blanket of the dark
To cry 'Hold, hold!'

Macbeth – Shakespeare.

Knives are not generally looked upon as lucky objects and are usually thought of as the tools of assassins. Because they are sharp

and can inflict a severe cut, or even a fatal wound, they should never be given as presents. They can cut friendship and must be bought, even if the price paid is nominal. The gift of a knife at Easter is thought to be doubly unlucky. If a knife happens to fall on the floor it is a sure sign that a visitor is coming, but if two knives should cross, be prepared for quarrels and arguments.

During the Middle Ages, however, knives were extremely acceptable presents. It was quite common for groomsmen to give them as a present to brides. She would then carry the knife at her wedding ceremony, in the same way that brides today often carry bouquets. In was thought that the knife would cut the groom's love if it was not true but would remain powerless for as long as he gave his devotion.

An old wive's tale along the East Coast of England says that if a knife is found in a baby's cradle it will bring good luck to the infant. This probably stems from an old Danish custom of hanging a bag containing rosemary, salt, bread and a knife over the cradle to welcome the baby when it was born.

Knives have long been symbols of bloody death, treachery and violence. They are a Christian symbol of martyrdom and, to the Buddhists, a stabber of demons.

Key Words and Phrases: tension, argument, danger from over-hastiness, treachery, deceit, underhand plotting, intrigues.

Subsidiary meanings:

Tension – worry, strain, unrest, discontent, stress, highly strung, forces pulling against each other, suppressed excitement likely to burst out.

Argument – disharmony, rift, bickering, friction, quarrels, feud, vendetta, clash, altercation, tiff, breaking point, area of disagreement, at loggerheads, fall out, part company, look for trouble, provoke, wrangle, row with.

Danger from over-hastiness – peril, vulnerability, expose oneself, run the risk, hang by a thread, come under fire, bode ill, hazardous, perilous, chancy, dicey, not safe, slippery, more haste less speed, unprepared, unorganized, snap, spur of the moment, undue urgency, in too much of a hurry.

Treachery/Deceit – double-dealing, doublecrossing, two-faced, dirty trick, perfidy, chicanery, sharp practice, unfaithful, traitorous, disloyal, shady, dishonest, deception, duplicity, fraud, tricks, lies, not what it seems, untrue, deceptive, play false, make an ass of, let down, leave in the lurch, catch out.

Underhand Plotting/Intrigues – stealthy, dishonest, misleading, crooked, bent, crafty, foxy, scheming, intriguing, not born yesterday, too clever by half, tricky, pull a fast one.

WHITE DICE – THREE SPOTS – HEART

Thou Lord hast made us for Thyself; therefore our hearts are restless until they rest in Thee.

—*St Augustine*

The heart, when employed as an emblem, signifies the centre of illumination and happiness. For this reason it is often portrayed surmounted by flames, a cross, a fleur-de-lis or a crown. Luckenbooths were special tokens (brooches, rings and so on) which were made during the seventeenth and eighteenth centuries in lock-up shops or booths in Edinburgh, hence the name. They were usually fashioned in silver and exchanged between sweethearts. They bore a heart-shaped emblem and sometimes two joined hearts surmounted by a crown.

Chambers, in his *Book of Days*, tells of another type of Celtic ring linked with the heart. Claddagh Rings come from the community of fisher folk living in Galway. They seldom intermarry and cling firmly to many old customs and beliefs. Their curious wedding rings bear the device of two clasped hands holding a heart. These rings have become heirlooms and are passed from mother to eldest daughter. The mother, apparently, ceases to wear a ring when her eldest daughter marries.

The Egyptians believed that the heart was the seat of the soul. It was the only part of the viscera left in the mummy since it was thought of as the centre, indispensible to the body in eternity. On the Day of Judgement they believed that the heart would be weighed and, if it passed the test, its owner would enjoy everlasting life and blessings. A cross resting on a heart was their symbol of goodness. The Egyptians also wore heart-shaped amulets as a protection against sorcerers who could charm the soul from the body. In Far Eastern philosophy the heart, together with the lotus flower and the rose, was viewed as symbolic of the hidden centre – 'hidden' because it is only imagined to exist. It denotes the state achieved through the elimination of separation.

When the body is viewed as a vertical scheme there are three focal points – the sexual organs, the heart and the brain. Because the heart is the central point it takes on the meanings of the other two.

Key Words and Phrases: love, affection, friendship, fondness, passion, desire.

Subsidiary meanings:

Love – desire, gives pleasure, want, need, passion, hunger for, fondness, infatuation, partiality, fascination, affinity, sexual desire, lust, attraction, unable to resist, true love, real thing, possessiveness, jealousy, fondness, liking, fancy, amorous, tender, attractive, charming, flirtation, amour, courtship, sweetheart, boyfriend, suitor, old flame, hold dear.

Friendship – amity, compatibility, fellowship, familiarity, intimacy, kindness, warmth, pal, mate, comrade, amicable, loyal, faithful, staunch, trustworthy, compatible, inseparable, thick as thieves, get pally, get acquainted.

WHITE DICE – TWO SPOTS – STORK

Constancy is like unto the stork, who wheresoever she fly cometh into no nest but her own.

— *Euphues – Lyly – 1580*

The stork has been viewed by all cultures as a bird of good omen. Storks build freely on the roofs of houses and outbuildings in Europe and, because they are regarded as lucky, they are not discouraged. In the Netherlands it is believed that no house will burn down while there are storks nesting on its roof, while the Chinese say that a house which harbours storks will not be robbed. Northern European children are told that the storks bring babies and drop them down the chimney. This is similar to the gooseberry bush story. Both the gooseberry and the stork are sacred to Venus, so a link in the stories can be found.

Storks are known to be excellent scavengers, besides waging war on all types of vermin. In the Middle Ages, when sanitation was almost unknown, storks were encouraged for the vital service they afforded to mankind. In China it was thought to be a bird which carried on the aims of forefathers and the Hebrews looked on it as a symbol of gratefulness, kindness, mercy and piety.

The stork is an aquatic bird – a fisher – and, because of its feeding habits, is associated symbolically with the waters of creation. It is known as the bringer of children which are found in embryo by the fishing storks in the creative waters of Mother Earth. The only derogatory belief attached to the stork is to be found in Chaucer's time when it was regarded as a symbol of adultery.

The stork received its name, according to a Swedish legend, from flying round the cross of the crucified Jesus crying 'Styrka! Styrka!' (strengthen! strengthen!).

Key Words and Phrases: new beginnings, ideas, projects, fertility, inventiveness, ingenuity.

Subsidiary meanings:

New Beginnings – not previously in existence, modern, recent, unheard of, up to date, revolutionary, move with the times, point at which things begin, source, origin, fresh starts, come into existence, enter on, embark upon, tackle, commence, set the ball rolling, take the plunge.

Ideas – notion, thought, concept, theory, percept, mental image, imagination, fancy, fantasy, brain wave, discovery, wheeze, contrive, reflection, observation.

Projects – plans, schemes, designs, organisation, programmes, proposal, strategy, programme of work, blueprints, plans of attack, approach to problem, schedule, devise.

Fertility – productiveness, booming economy, prosperity, fruitful, abundant, prolific, teeming, inventive, give birth, bring forth.

Inventiveness/Ingenuity – creativeness, all my own work, original, not imitation, uniqueness, independence, one's own, genuine article, first-hand, unimitated, thoughtful, brainwork, association of ideas, wily, foxy, dodge, wrinkle, little game, knowledgeable, canny, too clever for, know a trick or two.

WHITE DICE - ONE SPOT - SUN

The sun, centre and sire of light,
The keystone of the world-built arch of heaven.

Festus: Heaven — P. J. Bailey

The sun has gathered to itself many legends, beliefs and superstitions. Without the sun there would be no light or life in the world and it became the chief object of worship of many primitive peoples. The Egyptians saw it as Ra's golden boat sailing the sky, the Indians of Central America as the resting place of the dead and the Aborigines believed that it was created from an emu's egg which was tossed into the sky. The Hebrews saw it as symbolic of Jehova's might and it is also a Christian emblem of the Virgin Mary.

In astrology the sun governs the spirit, vitality, rulership, the will to live, organization and power. He is the ruler of the spirit, of the Zodiac sign of Leo, and the first day of the week – Sunday. The sun also has phallic attributes because of its procreative power and is thought of as a masculine force.

Primitive people regarded the sun as a wanderer making his endless journeys across the sky. He was also a life-giver because his arms (his rays) reached down to man and gave him the breath of life. Muspelheim is the name given in Norse mythology to a light and glowing land to the south and it was believed that the sun had

been sprayed from there into the heavens.

The sun is yet another dice symbol with Tarot links and, in this case, direct correspondences. The nineteenth card of the Tarot Trumps is called 'The Sun' and stands for glory, illumination, good health and success.

Key Words and Phrases: ambition, drive, forceful energy, success, power, achievement.

Subsidiary meanings:

Ambition – intention, calculation, purpose, determination, resolve, pursuit, project, design, desire, objective, hell-bent, out for, have in mind, intend for oneself, dream of, aspiration, expectation, vision, wishful, would-be, promise oneself.

Drive/Forceful Energy – vigour, power, force, energy, sparkle, fire, ardour, glow, enthusiasm, passion, powerful, nervous energy, bold, spirited, vivacious, impassioned, decisive.

Success – glory, happy ending, success story, time well spent, accomplishment, completion, triumph, victory, win the game, no defeat, master, effective, efficient, fruitful, profitable, unbeaten, make the grade, come off well, pull it off, bear fruit, crow over, get the better, win hands down, romp home, with flying colours.

Power – potency, control, sway, influence, ability, authority, manage, strength, force, superior, more than a match, compelling, have what it takes, prestige, leadership, government, lay down the law.

Achievement – gain, advance, headway, advancement, promotion, reaching goal, succeeding.

5
THE SYMBOLS OF THE GREEN DICE

GREEN DICE – SIX SPOTS – FRUIT-TREE

He that would have the fruit must climb the tree.

Gnomologia — Thomas Fuller No.2366

The symbol of the fruit tree has been replaced on modern sets of fortune dice by the pound or dollar sign but its significance remains the same – money, and all that it implies, as a reward for hard work. The fruit tree, as a symbol, was more appropriate in former times when farming communities regarded a good harvest of fruits as the reward for their labours throughout the year.

Different cultures have viewed the fruit tree and the fruit that it bears in various ways. In northern countries the apple figures heavily whilst in more southerly climes the orange, fig and grape vine are regarded as symbols of fruitfulness. In Chinese symbology fruit trees represent not only fertility but also longevity.

The tree itself represents life, growth, proliferation and the centre of the world. And because its roots spread out underground and its branches reach up towards the sky it symbolizes an upward trend. Fruit has been linked with the egg which is the seed of generation, the mystery of life. The apple features in the Adam and Eve story in the Old Testament when the first two people on earth were tempted by the serpent with an apple. It is linked with earthly desires and temptation. Which brings us back to the

modern day pound sign – money, one of the greatest earthly desires.

Key Words and Phrases: money, possessions, property, appearances, things worked for.

Subsidiary meanings:

Money – wealth, riches, luxury, opulence, affluence, solidity, substance, independence, resources, capital, fortune, well-heeled, flush, have the means, be able to pay, make ends meet, feather the nest, funds, cash, currency.

Possessions – ownership, belongings, rightfully owned, personal, one's own property, moveables, goods and chattels, belongings, effects, valuables.

Property – possessions, estate, assets, land, holdings, real estate, birthright, heritage.

Appearances – impressions created, externals, look of things, show, effect, visual impression, ostentation, how things seem, on the face of it, protocol, convention, custom, done thing, correctness, polish, manners.

Things worked for – desires, courses of action, ambition, aspiration, things that appeal, what has been achieved, gathered, earned.

GREEN DICE – FIVE SPOTS – GOBLET

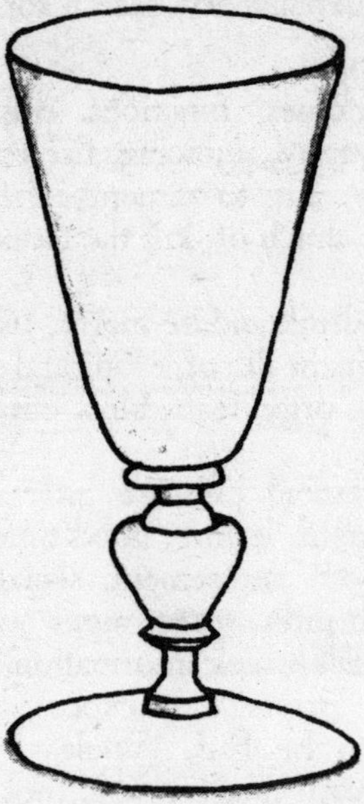

The goblet has the same symbolic meanings as the cup, which are – friendship, good fellowship, intuition, prudence and love. It is a symbol of the human heart. Because of its associations with the Holy Grail, of Arthurian Legend, it also represents a quest or the search for something. Although in their book *The Holy Blood and the Holy Grail* the authors (Michael Baigent, Richard Leigh and Henry Lincoln) assert that the grail was not a goblet but a bloodline.

The goblet, or chalice, has been widely used in religious ceremonies and is one of the main components of the Christian Communion Service. In other doctrines it has been used as a receptacle for the blood of a sacred king or deity. The symbolic links with the heart are carried on into the Tarot deck. 'Chalices' (goblets) was the name given to the heart suit which signified passion.

In Roman mythology it was associated with Mercury, the winged messenger of the gods, when in his role of leading the soul to unknown regions or presiding at birth.

Key Words and Phrases: celebrations, food and wine, entertainment, fun, debauchery, search for the unattainable.

Subsidiary meanings:

Celebrations – ceremonies, functions, occasions, do's, festive occasion, fête, festivity, rejoicing, fireworks, congratulations, toasts, special day, day to remember, field day, great day, anniversary, make much of, kill the fatted calf, do honour to, jubilations.

Food and wine – eat, drink and be merry, toast, pledge, drink to, raise glasses to, drink health of, eating and drinking, banqueting, wining and dining, orgy, feast, blow out, spread, good living, gourmet, epicure.

Entertainment – amusement, pleasure, interest, delight, diversion, relaxation, merriment, leisure, good time, round of pleasure.

Fun/Debauchery – sport, amusement, social gatherings, parties, feasts, revels, high jinks, spree, night out, frolic, prank.

Search for the unattainable – seek information, hunt, seek, look for, something whose presence is expected, investigate, quest, impossible, not to be had, hopeless, no chance, elusive, unavailable, too hard, unachievable, not feasible.

GREEN DICE – FOUR SPOTS – KEY

Mystery or enigma, the means to perform a task, threshold of the unconscious, access to knowledge – the key is symbolic of all these things. And to find a key signified the beginning of a difficult quest before the actual discovery of the treasure.

The key, as a symbol, is possibly even older than the Swastika which is regarded as being one of the earliest symbols employed by man. To the ancient Greeks and Romans the single key was an important mascot – it represented the Key of Life. These talismanic keys were made of silver, which was the metal of Diana. She, under her alias Jana, presided over the Threshold, although

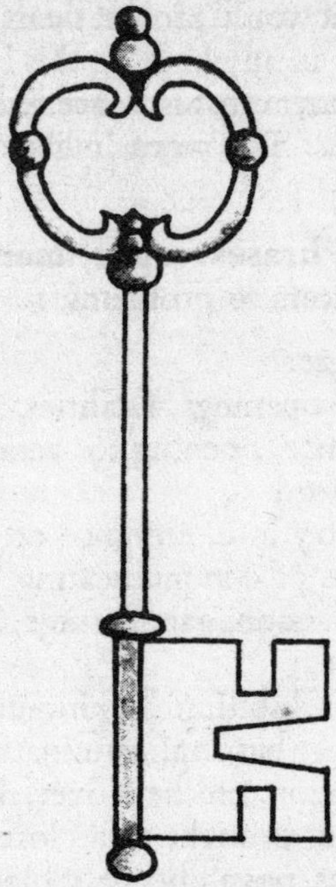

she was also joint custodian of the Doorway with her male counterpart Janus. She was also the guardian of child-bearing women and in this role kept watch over the Threshold of Life.

These talismanic keys were also closely connected with the Key of the Door through which the prayers of the devout reached the gods. They were a symbol of the entrance to Life and were worn to promote 'Remembrance of things past and foresight for things to come.' Sometimes their handles were heart-shaped and they became symbolic of guarded affection. They were given as love tokens – to lock or unlock the door of the heart.

The Greeks often wore the silver keys of Hecate attached to rings. This is another form of the Key of the Door symbolism. Hecate was the goddess of magical rites and of the underworld. She had power over the spirits of the dead and the key formed a link between the living and those departed. There is also a morphological connection between the Egyptian Nem Ankh sign – the anserated cross – the key of eternal life, which opens up the gates of death on to immortality.

The Romanies believed that if a door key was hung upside-down near their beds it would protect them from harm and ensure peaceful sleep. A ring of any kind, in this instance the ring at the top of the key, was a charm against Mare, the spirit of the night and bringer of bad dreams. The word 'nightmare' comes from this source.

Key Words and Phrases: opportunity, doors opening or closing, chances, answers to problems.

Subsidiary meanings:

Opportunity – chance, openings, facilities, free hand, favourable juncture, good chance, opening for action, to do, find, make, get, seize, give, afford.

Doors – threshold, entry into, entrance or exit, means of access, approach to, means of communicating.

Opening – chance for action, gap, passage, introduction, preface, beginning, entrance.

Closing – excluding, prohibiting, locking-out, preventing, disbar, shutting out, exiling, barring, terminating, ending, finishing, chance lost, completion, finished, over, no second chance, time up, come to an end, brought to a close, once and for all.

Chances – opportunities, possibility, gambles, risks, by chance, just happen, way things fall out, fortune, undesigned occurrences, fate.

Answers to problems – solutions, keys, clues, ways to solve, light, illumination, clarification, the secret, how to handle, what to do in the circumstances, – difficulties, worries, make one despair, complications, questions, something in need of solution, difficult to solve.

GREEN DICE – THREE SPOTS – LADDER

Alas! we make
A ladder of our thoughts, where angels step,
But sleep ourself at the foot: our high resolves
Look down upon our slumbering acts.

—*Landon*

The ladder is a very ancient symbol which represents ascension or the communication between different levels. Well into Victorian times, heaven was believed to be an actual country and the

Egyptians, particularly, thought that a ladder was necessary to reach this higher level of existence. Many Egyptian tombs have contained ladder-shaped amulets and one line from their *Book of the Dead* runs:

> My steps are now in position so that I may see the Gods.

These amulets were worn to supplicate the aid of Horus, the god of ladders, to leave behind all earthly things and to reach the greater heights. Some paintings discovered in the pyramids depicted two ladders. The first for the soul to climb out of the darkness of the grave and the second for the soul to ascend to the everlasting light.

The ladder features prominently in many religious teachings, and in Christianity it is seen as Jacob's Ladder with its seventy-two rungs reaching up into the clouds. Bettinis' *Libro del monte santo di Dio* (Florence 1477) depicts steps superimposed on a mountain. Each of the eleven rungs are named after a virtue – humility, prudence, temperance, fortitude, justice, awe, mercy, science, counsel, understanding and finally, wisdom.

The superstitious belief which still holds strong to this day, that it is unlucky to walk under a ladder, has its roots in the distant past. It is necessary to make a detour around the ladder to avoid disturbing, or indeed incurring the wrath of, any spirits who may be using it on their ascent to heaven. This superstition is reinforced by another piece of symbolism – a ladder when leant against a wall forms a triangle (the ladder, the wall and the ground) which was a symbol of life in olden times. Therefore it was thought extremely dangerous to walk beneath and break the imaginary triangle.

Key Words and Phrases: ambition, enthusiasm, new projects, ways up or down, up to you how you play things.

Subsidiary meanings:

Ambition – intention, calculation, purpose, determination, resolve, pursuit, project, design, desire, objective, hell-bent, out for, have in mind, intend for oneself, dream of, aspiration, expectation, vision, wishful, would-be, promise oneself.

Enthusiasm – ardent zeal, forceful energy, drive, vigour, power, force, sparkle, fire, ardour, glow, passion, nervous energy, spirited, vivacious, impassioned, decisive.

New Projects – not previously in existence, modern, recent, unheard of, up-to-date, revolutionary, move with the times, plans, conceptions, intentions, calculations, designs, schemes, proposals, objects, things to be done, strive after, aim at.

Ways up or down – courses, routes, methods, roads to take, means, potentials for, facilities, provide the route, course to a higher place, position, degree, amount, value, in an ascending direction/towards or to a lower or inferior place, level, position, state.

Up to you – your choice, what you make of it, nobody else can do things for you, you hold the controls.

GREEN DICE – TWO SPOTS – LIGHTNING

It is too rash, too unadvised, too sudden;
Too like the lightning, which does cease to be
'Ere one can say 'It lightens'.

Romeo and Juliet (Act II Sc 2) — Shakespeare

Lightning was, and still is, an awesome and frightening sight. It struck terror into the hearts of primitive man and many superstitions and beliefs have grown up around it. The Buddhists believed that the lightning god flashed in order to lighten the sky and enable the thunder god to take accurate aim to kill the wicked.

The Chinese revered it and regarded it as the dragon's tongue or the fire of heaven, and in Shivaism its flash was related to the glance from the third eye of Shiva, the destroyer of all material forms. This 'flash' has also been related to dawn and to illumination. The everyday sayings, 'It came to me in a flash' and, 'a sudden flash of inspiration', illustrate this aspect of lightning – that of inspiration and a glimpse of truth.

From a negative viewpoint lightning represents danger, destructive force – both terrible and dynamic – vengeance and, sometimes, it was believed to be the bringer of madness. The Tower Struck by Lightning, which is one of the Major Arcana cards in the Tarot pack, embodies some of these ideas. It alludes to the dangerous consequences of over-confidence (a destructive force) or the sin of pride, meglomania and the wild pursuit of fanciful ideas.

Jupiter was the Roman god associated with both lightning and thunderbolts. Oaks, which were believed to attract lightning more than any other tree, were consecrated to him in the hope that he would spare them from his wrath.

An ancient superstitious belief was that Earth had magical restorative powers because it provided life to plants and trees. If a man was struck by lightning he would be buried up to his neck in earth to ensure a rapid recovery from his ordeal.

The Hindus often wore a talisman which is best described as two arrow heads surrounded by cords which represented the thunderbolts of Indra, their weather god. It was carried to secure good fortune and to avert the influence of demons.

Key Words and Phrases: speed, hurry, quick actions, thoughtlessness, unexpected anger directed against you, wrong end of the stick.

Subsidiary meanings:

Speed – swiftness, quickness, greased lightning, move fast, tear, rush, flat out, in double time.

Hurry – move fast, bowl along, in double quick time, rush, no time to lose, break-neck speed, unable to wait, work against time, scurry, bustle, don't waste a minute, brook no delay.

Thoughtlessness – unthinking, inattentive, unwise, unreflective, mindless, not thinking, inconsiderate, careless, unseeing, rash, without consideration, foolish, miscalculated.

Unexpected Anger – surprise, shock, amazing, unguessed, unforseen, not anticipated, not bargained for, taken aback . . . resentment, displeasure, ill-humour, indignation, wrath, irritation, exasperation, hot displeasure, crossness, not amused, fury, burst of indignation, short temper.

Wrong end of the stick – misunderstanding, misinterpret, get wrong, blunder, not properly explained, not in the picture.

GREEN DICE – ONE SPOT – SNAIL

Like snails I see the people go
Along the pavement, row on row;
And each one on his shoulder bears
His coiling shell of petty cares –
The spiral of his own affairs.

From a Street Corner — Eleanor Hammond

The humble snail immediately conjures up a picture of a slow and clumsy creature dragging itself along the ground carrying its 'home' on its shoulders. To many it is a repulsive sight but mankind can learn an important lesson from the snail and his leisurely pace. In this high-speed world of the twentieth century leisure is an important commodity and certainly something which a snail has plenty of.

Snails have also been linked with concealment because of their ability to hide away in their shells when danger threatens. Taking this one step further – they have somewhere private to go where they are totally alone and can take stock of a situation before they re-emerge. Yet another lesson which we can benefit from – everyone needs somewhere to think, meditate and examine their problems quietly where they will not be disturbed.

Wherever a snail chooses to go he leaves a trail of slime behind him, he leaves his mark and will be remembered. The Celts called this trail the Light of the Lug. Lug was a Celtic deity of light, sky and the sun and Lug's Chain was the Celtic name for the Milky Way or track of souls. They drew parallels between this and the snail's earthly tracks.

Key Words and Phrases: health, slow up, care, think, on guard, no hurried decisions.

Subsidiary meanings:

Health – soundness of body and mind, good constitution, health and strength, fitness, condition, well-being, look after one's self.

Slow up – decelerate, reduce speed, ease up, take things easier, don't rush so much, rein in, moderate, take more time over things.

Care – attention to detail, keep an eye on, be vigilant, more meticulous, alert, on your toes, weather eye open, take care, watch what you're doing, look before you leap.

Think – use your brain, collect your thoughts, cogitate, meditate, contemplate, study, take stock, mull over, digest, examine, concentrate, ruminate, check things over first.

On Guard – vigilant, look out, surveilance, watchful, ready, prepared, attentive.

No hurried decisions – with undue haste, without reflection, on the spur of the moment, without thinking, settlements, conclusions, settle upon a course of action, plan of campaign.

6
HOW TO CAST

Three ordinary dice, each of a different colour, and a flat surface is all that you need for divining with dice. The three colours means that you can identify individual dice and, therefore, relate three lots of common numbers – the dots – to eighteen different symbols. The colours of the dice and the symbol linked with each face, are set out below:

First Dice – RED (which represents the hundreds)

Six	–	Bat
Five	–	Beetle
Four	–	Horseshoe
Three	–	Boat
Two	–	Skull
One	–	Web

Second Dice – WHITE (which represents the tens)

Six	–	Crossroads
Five	–	Cat
Four	–	Knife
Three	–	Heart
Two	–	Stork
One	–	Sun

Third Dice – GREEN (which represents the units)

Six	–	Fruit tree
Five	–	Goblet
Four	–	Key
Three	–	Ladder
Two	–	Lightning
One	–	Snail

You do not have to stay with this particular colour scheme (red/white/green) for your set of dice. But it is important that, once you have chosen your colours, you always interpret them in the same sequence.

Cast your three dice onto a flat surface and note the numbers of the dots on the uppermost faces. Repeat this twice more, noting the dots each time. At this stage, if you only want a quick and, therefore, very general interpretation to your casts, check the individual meanings in the final pages of this book.

The first dice throw will tell you about your (or your querent's) general situation. The second deals with financial and business matters and the third looks at love and affection. For more detailed readings you will also need to study the chapter on symbols and apply some of your own intuitive interpretations to the results.

There is another way to interpret these three casts but first you must decide whether you want a general reading, one with a financial slant or a reading concerning the affairs of the heart. Here you again cast the dice three times and note the numbers. But the first cast covers a period of three months hence, the second six months and the third a year. Look up each number in turn in the interpretations under the heading you have chosen and for more detail study the symbols and their meanings to add 'more meat to the bone'.

Your dice can also be used for short-term divination – the next seven days in fact – simply by totalling the number of spots and ignoring references to symbolic meanings. This is a very elementary method of divination by dice and the results achieved are basic and uncomplicated.

Cast the dice into a circle about seven inches in diameter drawn on a piece of paper. Should any dice roll out of the circle, or fall to the ground, they should be interpreted as follows:

One dice outside the circle – some difficulties, an upset of plans.
Two dice outside the circle – quarrels and arguments.
Three dice outside the circle – good fortune, a wish granted.
Dice which fall on the floor – annoyance and worry in the near future.

The spots on the uppermost faces of dice which have landed in the circle should be added up. If the total is less than three the dice have nothing to say. For a total of three or more spots the following interpretations apply:

Three – unexpected and surprising developments should occur almost immediately.

Four – unpleasantness and probably quarrels, discord and discontent.

Five – a wish will be granted, good news from a stranger or help from an unexpected quarter.

Six – discouragement, monetary loss or loss generally.

Seven – problems, difficulties to be overcome, business delays.

Eight – a thoughtless action can lead to trouble, reproach, criticism.

Nine – an engagement or marriage affecting the subject. Reconciliation.

Ten – female – a birth connected with the subject.
male – a promotion, or some new approach to a problem will be revealed.

Eleven – a loved one will make a journey, partings.

Twelve – an important letter – possibly containing good news, a message bringing the solution to a problem or relief of mind.

Thirteen – temporary unhappiness, sorrow if you continue with some matter in hand.

Fourteen – a friend will help you overcome a problem.

Fifteen – caution both in words and deeds to avoid trouble and problems.

Sixteen – a journey both pleasant and profitable terminating in happiness.

Seventeen – a change of mind, benefit from some matter to be concluded shortly.

Eighteen – success, rewards, happiness and almost immediate good fortune.

To gain further insight the circle can be divided into twelve equal segments radiating out from the centre, each of which should be labelled as follows:

1. The Home
2. Health
3. Wealth
4. Love/Happiness
5. Travel
6. Career
7. Legal Matters
8. Friends
9. Enemies
10. Hopes/Fears
11. The Present
12. The Future

Again three dice are cast into the circle and you should note any which fall outside. This time their numbers and meanings refer to the sections in which they land. The spots on each dice are interpreted as follows:

1. Favourable indications
2. Success depends on maintaining friendly relations
3. Triumph

4. Disappointment
5. Good news
6. Doubt

The spots from the three dice are then totalled for a general reading, as outlined.

7

SAMPLE CASTS

In the final section of this book you will find 648 individual meanings for 216 permutations of how dice can fall. Despite the numbers involved, these meanings can only be treated as very approximate guides. To a certain extent it is rather like the astrology columns in popular newspapers . . . you can hardly expect the day's comments for Leo or Aries to apply accurately to everyone born under those signs. Much the same applies here, in that the meanings are approximations. The secret of divination is that you, the reader, must apply some intuitive thought to any bald interpretations provided with divinatory casts or selections. To this end the meanings provided cannot wholly be treated as literal results. They should be studied in conjunction with the chapter on symbolism and then re-applied with your own intuitive judgements about your querent.

To illustrate how greater depth and clarity can be achieved from a cast of three dice (using intuitive assessments as well), here are six genuine case histories. Each of the querent's names have been changed for obvious reasons. But other details remain correct. In each case the results from the casts proved remarkably accurate. Before reading the results, however, it might be a good exercise to note the fall of the dice in each case, assemble details of individual meanings and symbolism and then, having read the background to each character, compare your own assessment with the authors'.

Sample One: Janet **Age:** 48

Occupation: Housewife
She is married to a man over ten years her junior. She has three children. She has an active interest in all matters to do with the occult and divination and has, on numerous occasions, attempted to get her work broadcast or published – so far with little success.

General Situation – **126 WEB STORK FRUIT-TREE**
This could be a rather disappointing period in Janet's life when things that inspire her and that she has been working towards do not seem to meet with the success and acclaim that she feels they really deserve. She will feel that someone has deliberately set out to take advantage of her. If it is not her money they try to trick her out of, then it will be her ideas or some discovery which she has made. There is, however, a bright side to look on and a new programme of work which she has not previously tried and, indeed, has only just thought of, will prove to be both profitable and rewarding.

Finance/Business – **136 WEB HEART FRUIT-TREE**
The business reading here seems to echo, to a great extent, most of what has already been said in the general reading. In fact, two thirds of both readings are exactly the same – the only change being that the Heart symbol takes the place of the Stork symbol in the first cast. The Heart in this case points to Janet being in love with her work and totally wrapped up in what she does. But however great the passion for her work, and however hard she tries to make an impression, she seems to be in a vulnerable position and surrounded by traps and pitfalls. She may even be guilty of self-deception and needs to look for some other way to earn money.

Love/Affection – **225 SKULL STORK GOBLET**
Janet's private life and home environment are about to undergo a sudden and rather unexpected change. She will have to adapt to this new situation and make alterations where necessary. This will be a time for fresh starts and a whole new chapter in her life. It will also be a time to celebrate and enjoy life more although she will have to keep on her toes to be one step ahead of other people. However, she must not lose sight of her own goals and ambitions during this period.

Sample Two: Martin **Age:** 29
Occupation: Public Speaker
Martin is happily married with one daughter and his interests and hobbies centre almost exclusively around his home. His working life is stressful and politically charged and could easily demand more, in time and effort, than he is prepared to give.

General Situation – **433 HORSESHOE HEART LADDER**
Life for Martin looks set to be very busy and enjoyable during the coming period. He will feel that he has found his feet and can afford to relax a little more and really begin to enjoy what he is doing. Plans to improve his home surroundings will show results and he will consider all his hard work and effort as time well spent. Company is very important to him and he will find himself involved in gatherings and social occasions, many of which will be impromptu and extremely entertaining. One particularly special family reason for celebration also seems likely.

He could find himself becoming more and more involved in some new and time-consuming interest which he had never dreamed possible. He will have to decide whether it is worth continuing quite so enthusiastically or whether there are other, more important, things to be done.

Finance/Business – **122 WEB STORK LIGHTNING**
Martin's business life looks extremely complicated – there are so many other spiders in the web in which he works all with their own little schemes and laying their own little traps for unsuspecting flies to get caught up in. He must endeavour to steer clear of office politics if he possibly can – no taking sides or getting involved in anything he's not sure about. He must be particularly wary of an extremely insincere person who will try to take advantage of his good nature and could land him in a spot of trouble.

He will have plenty of new ideas which he should push. However, when trying to do so he must ensure that he can answer any questions that may be asked. He must do his homework thoroughly and allow himself sufficient time to do things carefully and without error. Unreflective actions on his part could cause friction.

Love/Affection – **342 BOAT KNIFE LIGHTNING**
Martin's private life will have to take a back seat during the

coming months. There will be many things going on and much to be done – so, cosy evenings by the fire will have to be sacrificed. There could be many trips he will have to make at rather short notice, either alone or with his family, which will be particularly disruptive. Friction and areas of disagreement can be kept to a minimum if he remembers to give his wife plenty of notice about engagements and commitments which he undoubtedly will have.

Sample Three: Sylvia **Age:** 43
Occupation: Corporate Executive
Married without any children and totally devoted to her career. She has recently taken on new responsibilities in her working life. This new role has also meant rapidly learning new skills.

General Situation – **665 BAT CROSSROADS GOBLET**
Having reached a crossroads in her life when she has branched out and is feeling her way on unfamiliar territory, it's up to Sylvia to gather as much knowledge as possible about her new surroundings. She must not be afraid to ask questions or to seek information which will put her more fully in the picture. Once the initial confusion has passed she should be very happy and prosperous. Social functions and ceremonies are indicated which she will be expected to attend – sometimes in the role of hostess. One word of warning, however, there is someone she will come into contact with who is rather an unknown quantity. She should handle this person with care if she wants to avoid disagreements and confrontations. It's quite within this person's power to create trouble for her should they so decide. Her control over the situation will grow as time passes.

Finance/Business – **143 WEB KNIFE LADDER**
She is an ambitious person and is quite capable of reaching any objective once she has made up her mind to succeed. Syliva will find herself involved in new plans and projects which will revolutionize her place of work and provide a more modern approach to old ways of thinking. The sky is the limit for her provided she's not afraid of taking the controls and making decisions.

However, there are traps and pitfalls surrounding her which she could easily fall into and there are those around her who would be only too pleased to see her go wrong. She must be on her guard for potential trouble spots and also for people who are insincere, two-faced or just plain crafty. She is in a vulnerable position and must be well organized, well informed and on safe ground before she sticks her neck out. Above all – she must not make any hurried, spur of the moment decisions.

Love/Affection – **236 SKULL HEART FRUIT-TREE**
Sylvia's private life is due for major alterations which she had not bargained for and which will certainly leave her feeling rather taken aback. Life, as she has known it with her husband, is going to alter quite drastically and her old routines and way of living will be a thing of the past. This will be a change for the better and a move of home to a new area seems quite probable. Her new surroundings will be very impressive and something she has been hoping to achieve for some time. This will bring her nearer to close friends and loved ones.

Sample Four: Jeremy **Age:** 51
Occupation: Theatrical manager and performing arts organizer. Jeremy has two children from a former marriage. He has re-married but does not live with his children. He is exclusively involved in his work and is seeking new and prestigious avenues for development.

General Situation – **552 BEETLE CAT LIGHTNING**
There is a personal ambition which Jeremy has had in mind for some considerable time and which he has always promised himself he would get round to one day. Now is the time for him to do something about it. He must make up his mind to succeed and not allow obstacles or set-backs to put him off. This won't be an easy goal for him to reach but if he shows the necessary persistence and determination, and has the dedication to see it through, he will reach his target.

One of his children, or a relative, could cause him some problems in the coming months especially if they do something rather foolish and inconsiderate without consulting him first. His displeasure will be quite justified. It is quite possible that this disagreement will occur because of, or at, a family wedding or social gathering of some kind.

Finance/Business – **432 HORSESHOE HEART LIGHTNING**
Jeremy's business affairs look set to take off in a big way and an element of luck will certainly be with him. A joint venture with a close friend, probably of the opposite sex, looks possible, even if she only puts up the money and he does all the organization. Although he may not normally be tempted to take risks and try something speculative he must not dismiss an opportunity which will present itself soon simply because it seems chancy. Good luck will be with him especially in a gamble. He should have a go, as the outcome could be something of a breakthrough for him.

He must try not to get so wrapped in his haste to succeed that he becomes careless – he should always read the small print very carefully, especially if signing a contract. And if there is something which he is not quite sure about, he must ask questions. He would be very angry if he felt that he'd been deliberately misled.

Love/Affection – **521 BEETLE STORK SNAIL**
Jeremy and his wife must find time to sit down quietly together and talk over their plans for the future. They should take stock of what they have and decide just what they are both aiming for. He must not be afraid to consider new ideas, or to look for a fresh approach to an old problem – he may even want to move house. They should both avoid making hasty decisions, but once they have agreed on a course of action, they should stick to it.

Sample Five: Stephen **Age:** 21
Occupation: Student
Stephen is currently awaiting the results of his examinations so that he can decide whether or not to continue with his studies. He also needs to know whether he will be offered a grant. If his results are unfavourable, he will have to return home and seek employment. He has no current girlfriend.

General Situation – **121 WEB STORK SNAIL**
It is rather difficult for Stephen to make plans for his future until a problem which has caught him out, and proved to be a stumbling block, has been resolved. He cannot make any snap decisions at present and must spend his time studying, concentrating, and going over things in his mind to make sure that he knows what he's doing and is well prepared for the future.

Finance/Business – **644 BAT KNIFE KEY**
Working out his financial standing on anything but a short-term basis will not be possible at present. There is a shadow hanging over Stephen and until it has passed, and he can see exactly how he stands, long-term budgeting will have to be put to one side. If the outcome of this problem is good he will be able to continue as he is but if it is bad some rethinking will have to be done. Only the passing of time can throw light on his difficulties.

Love/Affection – **243 SKULL KNIFE LADDER**
Although Stephen is aware of the passing of time, and would like to establish a relationship with someone on more than a temporary basis, he seems hesitant and unsure of himself. He is afraid of being let down or appearing foolish in an intimate situation. There are also other worries and problems which have to be resolved in his life first. However, once he has put his life in order, and knows exactly what he is going to do and how he is going to spend the next few years, someone special will enter his life, quite suddenly and unexpectedly. This involvement will bring out a side of his character which has been lying dormant for years. He will also gain confidence in himself and will be able to handle new situations and challenges with ease.

Sample Six: Susan **Age:** 58
Occupation: Housewife and clerk
Susan is married with a grown-up family. Her husband's business is in difficulties and her own job is not very secure. The family depend upon her wages to remain solvent. She stretches herself to the limit and worries a great deal. Despite financial problems her marriage is happy.

General Situation – **351 BOAT CAT SNAIL**
Susan is very much the prop and stay of her family and their worries and problems are her worries and problems too. They all rely and depend on her a great deal so she must take great care of her health and guard against getting run down or depressed through overwork and stress. There is one particular problem which is worrying her and unfortunately there is no quick solution to it although she should still keep on the look out for ways round it. If this involves her job, it might be a good thing for her to seek employment elsewhere. She should ask around, make a few

telephone calls and see what other opportunities are open to her.

What she could really do with is a short holiday, or even a weekend away, to give her time to relax and recharge her batteries. She should try to visit relatives for a few days, the change would do her good.

Finance/Business – **231 SKULL HEART SNAIL**
As far as Susan's job is concerned, it's a case of here today and gone tomorrow, although she may be offered similar employment in another department or branch office if she works for a large organization. However, she would probably not want to take up this offer. She should be prepared to find herself out of work sooner than anticipated. This could be a blessing in disguise. A loved one will be instrumental in finding her new and better employment which she will not find quite so time-consuming or tiring.

Where her own money is concerned, she will have to manage this with care and avoid making any impulse purchases or buying items which she could do without. Thrift and frugality are the watchwords for her during the coming period.

Love/Affection – **416 HORSESHOE SUN FRUIT-TREE**
Her private life, which she shares with her husband, will be a source of great pleasure to her because they enjoy each other's company and are well suited. Susan's only problem area in her marriage is money. This is a matter they should face together rather than argue about. When she and her husband are both working together towards a particular goal they make a formidable team and always manage to succeed in the end, despite setbacks. However, they should try to avoid anything which seems risky or speculative. Her marriage should remain happy and contented.

8
INTERPRETATIONS

666 – BAT CROSSROADS FRUIT-TREE

General Situation: Annoyances and problems which have been dogging you lately have now run their course. A sudden, unepected jolt will help you to reach an important decision concerning a course of action which is open to you.

Finance/Business: Business matters have definitely been under a cloud recently but a turning point has now been reached and the opportunity to expand will be given to you by someone from outside your usual circle of acquaintances.

Love/Affection: There may have been some arguments between you and your partner which could well have been caused by new acquaintances. You must not air your differences in public – these disagreements will be solved in time.

665 – BAT CROSSROADS GOBLET

General Situation: Be on your guard concerning new friends you may meet at parties or other celebrations – they might have a few tricks up their sleeves which could catch you unawares.

Finance/Business: At work you could afford to relax a little as current, annoying problems will soon be ironed out. Prosperity is just around the corner bringing with it an opportunity to achieve something you have always wanted.

Love/Affection: Try not to make a fool of yourself over someone new you might meet. Forewarned is forearmed.

664 – BAT CROSSROADS KEY

General Situation: Don't allow other people to influence an important decision you will soon have to make. It could be very much to your advantage, but someone who is feeling envious might try to give you dubious advice. You know how to handle the situation. Remember an opportunity like this will not be repeated.

Finance/Business: Opportunity knocks – but will it be to your advantage or will it be more trouble than it's worth? Before you commit yourself financially make sure that there are no hidden surprises. But don't take too long or you may miss your chance.

Love/Affection: If things between you and your partner have been a little stormy lately don't despair, it will pass. Circumstances are about to change and a new and better understanding will develop between you.

663 – BAT CROSSROADS LADDER

General Situation: The opportunity you have been waiting for to pursue a personal ambition is just around the corner and will be revealed to you soon. It could prove to be a turning point in your life and the onus is on you to make the most of this chance. Use your ideas and energy towards a positive end and don't be afraid to be inventive and revolutionary in your ideas.

Finance/Business: The sun is beginning to shine again on your business dealings bringing with it a few surprises which you are not prepared for. A decision will have to be taken which could see you a few rungs higher up the ladder of success.

Love/Affection: You are mistaken if you think that a friendship you are cultivating could bring with it any financial reward. Try not to mix business with pleasure, this is not a good idea.

662 – BAT CROSSROADS LIGHTNING

General Situation: Look before you leap! Don't go making any important decisions without prior consultation with your family or you may find misunderstandings will arise and tempers will become frayed. Put all your cards on the table, think things out very carefully and keep everyone in the picture.

Finance/Business: Where finances are concerned – it would be better to do nothing than to enter into any agreement without first making very careful calculations and studying the viability of the scheme. Good communications must be maintained to keep everyone fully informed and good-humoured.

Love/Affection: Say what you mean – your partner isn't a mind-reader. Don't hide your intentions. The only surprise you should spring is a little present bought on impulse.

661 – BAT CROSSROADS SNAIL

General Situation: You may not be feeling all that well or energetic but things will soon improve as long as you don't try to take on more than you can manage. Slow down a little and take more time to relax. Learn to delegate more often.

Finance/Business: Don't come to any hasty decisions over a business matter. Your resources may be very tightly stretched and any extra strain could prove troublesome. Delay matters for a while and wait until your financial situation improves before taking on any more commitments.

Love/Affection: Don't allow jealousy to cloud matters. Let them run their course and avoid any spur-of-the-moment decisions. There is a surprise in store for you which will certainly be an eye-opener.

656 – BAT CAT FRUIT TREE

General Situation: Family matters and finances have definitely been under a considerable strain during the past months. Fortunately, this run of bad luck is coming to an end and things can only get better. Try not to let it get you down too much.

Finance/Business: Your best plan of action, at present, is to just carry on with the day-to-day administration of your business life and avoid trying anything new or different until financial conditions show some marked improvement.

Love/Affection: Your relationship with your partner seems to have been overshadowed by business worries and problems which you have probably taken home with you. This is only a passing phase. Have you tried sharing your troubles instead of bottling them up?

655 – BAT CAT GOBLET

General Situation: It's just a matter of time before those dark days will be gone for good and you and your family will have cause for celebration. Make the most of life and find time to relax and enjoy yourselves. How about a family holiday somewhere exotic?

Finance/Business: At last things seem to be getting back on to an even keel again and your bank balance is more often black than red. Why not celebrate a little and have a night out with your workmates?

Love/Affection: A family wedding or anniversary celebration is indicated and a passing stroke of good luck will provide the icing on the cake. Get together and have fun.

654 – BAT CAT KEY

General Situation: A windfall will provide you and your family with just the opportunity you have all been waiting for. Make the most of this chance as it could help you out of what has been a worrying situation.

Finance/Business: Financial worries will be a thing of the past if you seize a chance that will soon be offered to you. It will provide the way into a whole new field of operation and also chances and introductions hitherto denied to you.

Love/Affection: A chance meeting for single people could lead to a whole lot more than bargained for. Be ready to seize opportunities and let your feelings be known.

653 – BAT CAT LADDER

General Situation: Troubles appear to be behind you now and the future seems promising. You will have lots of new opportunities, plans and ideas and the energy and will to tackle them. Life will be what you make of it.

Finance/Business: Events behind the scenes have altered circumstances and the chance of promotion is there if you want to take it. A new venture will provide just the opportunity you have been waiting for – something which no one else has the expertise to handle but you.

Love/Affection: You and your partner will now be able to do something which you have always dreamed of together. This new scheme will bring you closer together and will be very rewarding.

652 – BAT CAT LIGHTNING

General Situation: If you are wondering why your family seem to be irritated with you lately it is because they have misunderstood something which you have done. Take the time to explain and don't be in such a hurry in future.

Finance/Business: A business venture involving your family will need careful handling if quarrels and rows are to be avoided. Don't try to do things too quickly and make sure that everyone knows what is expected of them. Preliminary teething troubles will soon be ironed out.

Love/Affection: Don't go flying off the handle at your partner until you are sure you know what you're talking about. You may not be aware of all the facts and could appear a little foolish if you react too quickly.

651 – BAT CAT SNAIL

General Situation: A bad period you are going through which will pass soon, but it is putting extra pressure on your family. You must slow up and take more time to relax.

Finance/Business: This is definitely not the right time to make any important decisions. There are other worries and problems you will need to deal with first. Wait until you have time to discuss matters with your family and don't take on any extra responsibilities for the moment.

Love/Affection: Try to find a little more time to devote to your partner who may be feeling neglected. Don't let your feelings be suppressed because of other things on your mind. Try to be more demonstrative.

646 – BAT KNIFE FRUIT-TREE

General Situation: This could be an unpleasant time for you. Your home and possessions might seem threatened and the strain and tension you are under could be quite considerable. Certain friends are not to be trusted and any hasty actions on your part would only exacerbate the situation. One word of consolation, this is only a temporary state of affairs and in due course things will get back on to a more steady footing again.

Finance/Business: Do nothing, decide nothing, trust no one. It is likely you are surrounded by extremely bad circumstances which threaten your financial position. Try to keep a cool head and ride out of the storm – it will abate eventually.

Love/Affection: Keep an eye on the amount of money your partner is spending and you will save yourself a lot of unpleasantness. Maybe find out what it is that they want to buy so badly and buy it for them.

645 – BAT KNIFE GOBLET

General Situation: Don't allow others to trick you into doing something you really don't want to do. They are not such good friends at all, but are only trying to make you appear stupid. It could be something simple like someone doctoring your drink at a party.

Finance/Business: Don't be too eager to get involved in other peoples' financial schemes even though they may have wined and dined you royally and you feel under an obligation to go along with their plans.

Love/Affection: A quiet candlelit meal for two would be a good way of forgetting an argument and will give you the chance to talk things over with your partner on neutral ground.

644 – BAT KNIFE KEY

General Situation: You might have been feeling uncertain of yourself recently but this will pass. Be careful how you handle matters and under no circumstances act without careful thought.

Finance/Business: This is not the right time for any kind of speculative enterprise but don't just sit there idling away your time. Use this period to calculate your next move.

Love/Affection: You will have the opportunity to meet new people and make new friends but be a little on your guard as a new relationship which may spring up could cause friction and quarrels. It will not be long term.

643 – BAT KNIFE LADDER

General Situation: Something which you have been planning to do for some time is in danger of being sabotaged, not only by your own over-hastiness, but also by someone else who will let you down at the last moment. Avoid possible disappointment by thinking things over and make sure that you are fully in control.

Finance/Business: As fast as you seem to achieve something financially, problems crop up which put you back to square one. In the meantime don't let it get you down and don't try to run before you can walk.

Love/Affection: Your current relationship is going well but don't try to push matters or you could provoke an argument. Tread very carefully if you wish to succeed.

642 – BAT KNIFE LIGHTNING

General Situation: Your best plan of action would be to stay at home with a good book. It seems everything you do goes wrong. It could be your own fault or others working against you. Keep a low profile.

Finance/Business: Be prepared to act quickly. A deal clinched now will be advantageous although colleagues may be taken aback by this fast move and fail to understand your motives.

Love/Affection: Your love life seems confused to say the least at present. Try to be a little more considerate or you could find yourself facing an ill-humoured partner.

641 – BAT KNIFE SNAIL

General Situation: Now is the time to take a break, slow the pace and spoil yourself a little. Give your body a chance to recover after all the strain you've been under lately. Collect your thoughts. By mulling things over you will be able to get a clearer picture of the future.

Finance/Business: Pressure of work seems to be getting you down and just when you need the support and loyalty of colleagues they are too busy with their own schemes and let you down. These problems will not undermine your health if you take your time and get yourself organized.

Love/Affection: Don't let family feuding and quarrels come between you and your partner. Their bickering could well force some decisions upon you that you are not prepared for. Be honest with each other and if it's snap decisions they want, they'll just have to wait while you consider things.

636 – BAT HEART FRUIT-TREE

General Situation: The impression you create to others seems to be very important to you. Try to play down your desire to impress, as your real friends like you for who you are and not what you have.

Finance/Business: An office romance is not really a very good idea, beside distracting you from your work it could cause all sorts of other problems too. You have worked hard for the position you now hold so don't throw it all away because of a moment of weakness.

Love/Affection: Your partner has suddenly decided to 'keep up with the Jones's' – to your cost. Avoid spending too much money on appearances.

635 – BAT HEART GOBLET

General Situation: Good times are coming and the austere conditions you have been living under will give way to one long round of pleasure and amusement. So eat, drink and be merry while it lasts.

Finance/Business: While caution has been the watchword in the past, now is the time to splash out a little and prove to others that you're not such a mean old Scrooge as they thought.

Love/Affection: A wonderful time ahead for you and your partner to relax and enjoy some good living together, and some good loving too! Single people need not frown either – parties, high jinks and love.

634 – BAT HEART KEY

General Situation: Old troubles and problems which you feel have been holding you back have run their course and you are entering a phase full of good opportunities and new beginnings in both your private and professional life.

Finance/Business: If your finances have given you cause for despair in the past – take heart, a close friend will provide you with just the opportunity you have been waiting for to capitalize.

Love/Affection: If you have been feeling a little unloved of late that will certainly not be the complaint now. Friends will rally round and take you out of yourself. An existing relationship will get back onto a better footing or a new involvement seems bound for success.

633 – BAT HEART LADDER

General Situation: Friends could help you to achieve an ambition which you have had for some time. However, success is usually that much sweeter if you have achieved it by yourself. You should find that friends won't mind 'passing the reins over' for a while.

Finance/Business: The chance to make a profit will come from a most unexpected quarter. However, if you let this stroke of good luck go to your head you may lose friends.

Love/Affection: Try not to take advantage of your partner's good nature. it won't help you in the long run and will only serve to alienate them.

632 – BAT HEART LIGHTNING

General Situation: Think before you speak or you could find yourself on your own. Unless you choose your words with care, misunderstandings and acrimony will be the result.

Finance/Business: An outstanding debt that really ought to be paid off could soon be settled if you pushed yourself just a little more – maybe even do a bit of overtime.

Love/Affection: A sudden love or infatuation is probable but whatever you do, don't get too involved as it will alienate your family and gain your friend's disapproval.

631 – BAT HEART SNAIL

General Situation: Where's the fire? All this hurry and haste is really not good for you and healthwise it's already beginning to show. If it's really so important to get things done quickly why not enlist the help of family and friends.

Finance/Business: Overwork and poor health go hand in hand unless you slow up. Delegate more so that you are well enough to enjoy the financial benefits you seem almost certain to reap.

Love/Affection: Don't keep trying to hurry your partner or you could find yourself very much on your own. Instead, let them have their own way a little more and things will show a marked improvement and be happier.

626 – BAT STORK FRUIT-TREE

General Situation: The past and its troubles and worries are a closed chapter. The accent is now on the future and what you make of it. Take the plunge and launch that new idea of yours – it should prove to be a great success.

Finance/Business: That get rich quick idea of yours may not be as outlandish as you first thought. Get some capital behind you (either yours or someone else's) and give it a try. Success is assured and the rewards could be great.

Love/Affection: Your partner has been nursing an ambition for quite a while and the only thing holding them back is funds, or rather lack of them. Give them encouragement and a little financial backing – if you can afford it at present.

625 – BAT STORK GOBLET

General Situation: New projects which you are working on seem to be temporarily dogged by bad luck. Teething troubles abound and just when things are taking shape something else seems to go wrong. These are only passing set-backs and success will be achieved by your own inventiveness and ingenuity. What you do will not go unnoticed.

Finance/Business: It would be a good idea to entertain business associates in order to promote new interests and collect new ideas. Your mind is particularly fertile at present and you may need to seek backing for your schemes which could be best discussed over a meal. Past hindrances are definitely going.

Love/Affection: Any feelings of despondency between you and your partner are going and relationships will get on to a much more stable basis. A birth or christening in the family is possible.

624 – BAT STORK KEY

General Situation: Aches, pains and headaches which have been with you for some time will go because you will be too busy to sit and worry about how you are feeling. This is a time to be creative and develop new ideas, to seek new approaches and to decide new plans of attack. Don't waste it.

Finance/Business: So long as you handle things in the right manner financial problems should be relatively easy to solve. New fund-raising opportunities should be taken when they arise.

Love/Affection: For single people this is not a time to make any proposals concerning the future as there are still past problems to be resolved. Those of you with partners should try to confess something which you have been holding back.

623 – BAT STORK LADDER

General Situation: Stop champing at the bit to get started on new projects. Make sure that your ideas really are viable before you put them to the test. Failure would be unthinkable, so think first – act later.

Finance/Business: If you would only let bygones be bygones you would be able to make more headway in your career. The opportunities are there and you certainly don't lack determination or drive, so forget whatever it is that still wrankles and allow yourself to move with the times.

Love/Affection: Your partner could be extremely irritating. Try to ignore it as much as you can, it will pass. Get on with something you are interested in instead.

622 – BAT STORK LIGHTNING

General Situation: You could probably do with some strenuous exercise – it will help get rid of some of those daily frustrations. Muddles and irksome little problems will exasperate you and if only people would say what they mean life would be much easier. Get these irritations sorted out as soon as you can, then put your mind to more creative use.

Finance/Business: Speculate – but move swiftly, there's no time to lose. Buy at once and be assured of a nice profit when you re-sell.

Love/Affection: Perhaps some private worry has made you a little hesitant when it comes to showing your affections. Remember – he who hesitates is lost. Go ahead and do something positive, you'll be surprised what an effect it will have.

621 – BAT STORK SNAIL

General Situation: You should be feeling in fine fettle at the moment but don't go rocking the boat by getting overtired. Your mind seems to be working overtime and you are full of original ideas and thoughts. Remember that you can't do everything at once.

Finance/Business: A new financial venture stands a good chance of success but don't go counting your chickens too early as quite a lot of things could go wrong if you hurry matters. Time will tell.

Love/Affection: Spend more time with your partner instead of rushing about from one social engagement to another. Put your heads together and make a few positive future plans for just the two of you.

616 – BAT SUN FRUIT-TREE

General Situation: Fate is really giving you a helping hand and you don't seem to be able to put a foot wrong. Whatever you touch is bound to succeed. Go ahead and enjoy yourself.

Finance/Business: The Midas touch is yours – go ahead with your money-making plans and schemes, they really can't fail. Promotion and greater responsibility could be offered which will also bring with it financial gain.

Love/Affection: Come down to earth or you will drive your partner mad. It's all very well to be a walking success story but when you've heard the story for about the third time in one evening it can become more than a little irritating.

615 – BAT SUN GOBLET

General Situation: Hold on – you're so busy trying to get on in the world and doing very well at it that you haven't had a night out for a long time. Why not treat yourself to a visit to the cinema, a meal or maybe even a weekend away visiting friends.

Finance/Business: Don't become too over-confident just because things are really booming for you. Even you can put a foot wrong and a social gaff while out dining with the boss and important clients would not go down very well.

Love/Affection: Be satisfied with what you have, if your partner loves and respects you, what more do you want? It's no good spoiling what you have by searching for something which only exists in your mind.

614 – BAT SUN KEY

General Situation: You hold the key to not only your own pleasure but to the pleasure of those dependent upon you. Don't let something in your past spoil your dreams for the future.

Finance/Business: An acceptable way out of a tricky financial problem is at hand. Try to learn from your mistakes and you shouldn't go wrong again. Examination results will be good.

Love/Affection: Kiss and make up. Your future is with your partner and you must learn to handle problems between you. You can't always be right.

613 – BAT SUN LADDER

General Situation: This is a very favourable time to pursue a long held ambition. You are full of energy and determination and as long as you stay in control of the situation your efforts will be rewarded. Don't allow a ghost from your past to mar your success.

Finance/Business: You are more likely to succeed than to fail but this is no reason to be over-confident and take unnecessary risks. Remember that nothing is one hundred per cent certain until it has been achieved.

Love/Affection: This is a particularly special time for lovers and should you be thinking of marriage now is the time to start making plans. If already married how about a second honeymoon?

612 – BAT SUN LIGHTNING

General Situation: Be prepared to act extremely quickly but not inconsiderately if you want to make the most of an opportunity for advancement which will occur soon. Should something be worrying you healthwise don't keep it to yourself but have it checked out. You will save yourself a lot of needless worry.

Finance/Business: This tendency you have to do everything at break-neck speed could mean that you may miss a golden opportunity.

Love/Affection: What have you been up to that's put you in your partner's bad books again? You really must show more consideration and be a little more caring. How about a little surprise present to show that you do stop and think sometimes.

611 – BAT SUN SNAIL

General Situation: If you really bother to collect your thoughts for just a moment and act with just a little more care and wisdom you will see that it is quite possible to overcome something which has been worrying you lately. Look before you leap and think before you act.

Finance/Business: Fortune is smiling on your affairs and seeds you had sown some time ago are now bearing fruit. However, don't try to harvest everything at once or a few of these fruit could get damaged in the process.

Love/Affection: Your partner may be feeling a little tired and under the weather. Use some of your excess energy to help them out until they can get back on their feet again.

566 – BEETLE CROSSROADS FRUIT-TREE

General Situation: A specific ambition which you have been relentlessly pursuing will bring a sudden surprise. A person from outside your direct family circle could spring on you an offer which could bring benefits.

Finance/Business: Hard work is finally going to pay dividends. A sudden chance decision taken over something you have been working on will bring financial rewards which will benefit not only you, but those close to you.

Love/Affection: Go ahead with ideas which may mean some financial outlay. This is a wise thing to do and will be much appreciated by your partner.

565 – BEETLE CROSSROADS GOBLET

General Situation: Don't go turning down social invitations because of your dedication to duty. Everyone needs to allow themselves a little time to relax, see friends and pursue hobbies. Is there someone who can deputize for you for a while?

Finance/Business: It's really been a long, hard struggle to get your latest venture off the ground and only your tireless patience has made it work. Take a breather before you get wrapped up in any new project.

Love/Affection: Why not treat your partner to something a little special – it's rather nice to have a surprise treat occasionally and you could do with a little diversion too. Make it an occasion to be looked back on with pleasure.

564 – BEETLE CROSSROADS KEY

General Situation: All that hard work and study you did when everyone else was out enjoying themselves is about to pay off in a most unexpected way. You will be at a crossroads in your life and you will have to decide on a course of action and stick to it.

Finance/Business: An unexpected windfall could provide you with financial security and put you back on your feet again. Pay off all those worrying outstanding debts and keep a tighter grip on your purse strings in future.

Love/Affection: Don't go feeling unloved and unlovable, affection for you is there but it may not necessarily be shown as you would like. Give it a chance – it'll come out eventually.

563 – BEETLE CROSSROADS LADDER

General Situation: If anyone deserves recognition for sheer hard work, you do. Your salvation will come from a most unexpected quarter but don't let that worry you. Convert your dreams into realities and make the most of a very good offer you are sure to receive soon.

Finance/Business: It's all very well being ambitious but the only way you will climb the ladder of success is by lots of hard work, repeated efforts and resolution. You can do it and the rewards are great.

Love/Affection: The old love life looks in for a stormy time, try to find out if relatives have been interfering again. It's surprising how much trouble can be stirred up by a seemingly harmless remark. A move of house to another area might help.

562 – BEETLE CROSSROADS LIGHTNING

General Situation: Are you really surprised that your family are complaining? Try not to get so involved in a new hobby or other interest that you don't have time for anything or anyone else. Try to be a little less thoughtless and you could be in for a few pleasant surprises.

Finance/Business: A new workmate or colleague could well be the cause of disputes and arguments amongst those you work with. You would be well advised not to get involved or this could make matters worse and even upset your own future plans and ambitions.

Love/Affection: Someone close to you is about to make a revelation you had not bargained for. Make sure that you understand what they want as a misunderstanding over this could result in short tempers and ill-humour all round.

561 – BEETLE CROSSROADS SNAIL

General Situation: A surprise opportunity will need a great deal of thought and a thorough checking out before you reach a decision. If the general everyday pressures of life seem to be weighing a little heavily on you at present, try to keep calm and deal with them one step at a time.

Finance/Business: You could be in for a very pleasant surprise which you certainly had not bargained for. It could be to do with money or property but is more likely to be concerned with a more intimate article such as a piece of jewellery or an item of furniture.

Love/Affection: You really must stop being so romantic and with your head in the clouds where your affections are concerned. Take time to weigh things up and be a little more materialistic in your future approach to personal situations.

556 – BEETLE CAT FRUIT-TREE

General Situation: Try not to feel too despondent and that you will never get all the things you are working so hard for. Talk things over with your family – you may be able to enlist their help or get some new ideas from them. Keep at it, you really can do it.

Finance/Business: As far as income is concerned this is a really good time for you and things are ticking over nicely. Put your efforts into long-term projects rather than trying any get-rich-quick schemes which could prove to be your downfall.

Love/Affection: People around you would seem to be getting more out of life than you. Take a really good look at what you have going for you and you'll be surprised how much you take for granted. Get your values straight.

555 – BEETLE CAT GOBLET

General Situation: You and your family really do have something to celebrate – all that hard work and dedication will now start to pay off.

Finance/Business: Everyone else may have said that your project was doomed from the start but your determination and 'never say die' attitude has proved them all wrong. Resist the temptation to crow about it but by all means enjoy your much deserved success.

Love/Affection: Put a little romance back into your life, perhaps a candlelit supper for two at a nice intimate little restaurant or even a special supper at home with your partner – soft lights and soft music are a must now.

554 – BEETLE CAT KEY

General Situation: Help is at hand, and a problem which you have found difficult to solve will then be seen in a different light. Try to be a little more cheerful as a new phase in your life is coming which will be full of good opportunities.

Finance/Business: Your own financial worries and problems will have to take second place for the time being as someone in your family circle will need your help and advice about a tricky situation they are in. You'll be glad you bothered.

Love/Affection: Don't try quite so hard to impress people and make them like you. Just try being yourself for a change. You'll be surprised what a difference it will make.

553 – BEETLE CAT LADDER

General Situation: This is what you've been waiting so long for – your chance for success. However, you must play your cards very close to your chest as there's always someone who will steal your ideas if they get a chance.

Finance/Business: Money matters are definitely showing an upwards trend at long last. However, it would not be advisable to go buying something frivolous and expensive, at this time.

Love/Affection: You may be faced with making a choice between what your partner wants and your own personal ambition. Allow common-sense to rule the situation.

552 – BEETLE CAT LIGHTNING

General Situation: A niggling little health problem which has been with you for some time will seem to improve overnight. Also now is the time to solve a personal problem provided that you act swiftly but not foolishly.

Finance/Business: This is a lesson that everyone has to learn at some time in their lives – you can't expect to get something you want and give nothing in return. The only way to get what you want is by sheer hard work.

Love/Affection: Emotionally you're in for a very busy time, and if you are happy with how things are going then encourage them, but don't delay too long as indecision from you may be mistaken for indifference.

551 – BEETLE CAT SNAIL

General Situation: Although other people, particularly your family, may seem to be interfering with or hindering your plans, try not to let this annoy you too much. After all, if you actually think over what they have been saying, you might find they have a point.

Finance/Business: Now is a time to formulate new ideas and think about new projects but seek professional advice before you take any definite steps. You may not agree with the advice but don't dismiss it out of hand.

Love/Affection: Be a little more patient as far as your partner is concerned. Other people have feelings too although they may not be the same as yours on every subject. Guard against spur of the moment actions, it's not worth the risk.

546 – BEETLE KNIFE FRUIT-TREE

General Situation: Do you ever get that feeling that someone is being friendly because of what you have rather than who you are? Try to find out who it is and make sure you are not being deceived.

Finance/Business: However persuasive those salesmen are and however foolproof their schemes might seem, don't invest any money unless you have essential guarantees.

Love/Affection: Although your partner may seem a little dull at times, stick with that one however sorely tempted you may be. After all it is better the devil you know than the devil you don't.

545 – BEETLE KNIFE GOBLET

General Situation: Try not to rely too much on others as you could be let down at a time when you most need that extra pair of hands to see you through. Instead, rein in a little and keep matters very much under your own control.

Finance/Business: At first glance everything seems to be in order and running well but there is still an underlying feeling that all is not as it should be. Check up on figure work and, if appropriate, do a bit of stocktaking too.

Love/Affection: Don't do anything that might rock the boat. Things are going very nicely between you and your partner and it would be a pity to spoil this mood of good will.

544 – BEETLE KNIFE KEY

General Situation: Your chance is coming to settle old scores with someone who has repeatedly let you down in the past. Something has to be done to clear the air and settle past complaints once and for all.

Finance/Business: Don't be tempted to use others in order to gain your own ends financially. It's not a good idea and one which could quite easily backfire with disastrous results.

Love/Affection: If your partner should somehow upset you try not to over-react and fall out over it. It was not done with the intention to deceive and is better off forgotten.

543 – BEETLE KNIFE LADDER

General Situation: Your unbending desire to reach a personal goal could lead you into dangerous territory. Try not to annoy others and just for once take 'no' for an answer and be satisfied. Make the effort to be more thoughtful for a change.

Finance/Business; How about helping someone else out for a change as you can quite easily afford it at present. You'll be surprised what a rewarding experience it can be!

Love/Affection: Instead of worrying about whether your partner is somehow losing interest in you, it would be a good idea to be a little more demonstrative yourself. You know how you feel but how long is it since you last told them. it could well ease the tension you have both been feeling of late.

542 – BEETLE KNIFE LIGHTNING

General Situation: Avoid arguments if you can at the moment.

What you really ought to do is to slow down and take things a little easier – tiredness and strain from overworking could affect your health in the long term.

Finance/Business: Don't allow a colleague to trick you into doing something on the spur of the moment for which you are not prepared. This will only lead to misunderstandings because you were not properly briefed.

Love/Affection: You ought to pay attention to what your partner has to say or you could find yourself in the wrong. Make every effort to understand what he or she really means.

541 – BEETLE KNIFE SNAIL

General Situation: It would be a good idea to keep complaints to yourself for the time being. Make sure that you really do have a valid grievance before you air it.

Finance/Business; You may find yourself a little behind with payments or instalments of some sort. You must not let this worry you as it will be possible to catch up again although this is something which cannot be done quickly.

Love/Affection: If your partner seems to be feeling a bit cantankerous and quarrelsome; make sure that it's not you who gets the rough edge of their tongue. Keep your head down and wait for the storm to pass.

536 – BEETLE HEART FRUIT-TREE

General Situation: Get out of the rat race for five minutes and spend some time with your family and friends. The indications are that you all need a short holiday.

Finance/Business: Just this once it might not be a bad thing to let your heart be your guide in a business venture instead of going by the book. Use your intuition.

Love/Affection: You and your partner should let your hair down and enjoy yourselves instead of always being conventional. Be a little outrageous – it could be fun!

535 – BEETLE HEART GOBLET

General Situation: Pleasant and happy times are in store for you in the company of your family and close friends. Enjoy life to the full and grab opportunities to celebrate when they present themselves.

Finance/Business: Your advice on a financial matter will be sought by a friend and should not be given grudgingly. You never know when you may need help one day.

Love/Affection: You and your partner will be feeling very much in tune during the coming period. Your relationship will seem to strengthen and become more exciting.

534 – BEETLE HEART KEY

General Situation: Just when you were beginning to despair of ever solving some longstanding problems a friend will point you in the right direction to succeed. From then on it's up to you.

Finance/Business: Have you ever considered going into partnership with a friend? You should, as a chance to do so will arise very soon and the rewards could be considerable provided that you both pull together.

Love/Affection: Someone who you once regarded as being very special is about to come back into your life. This will mean not only new opportunities but a few problems too.

533 – BEETLE HEART LADDER

General Situation: There are things to be done, new plans to be made and fresh targets to aim for. And you have plenty of friends who are only too willing to lend a hand and get you started.

Finance/Business: Financial security is always something which you have aimed at. You will have to make a choice about a new career which could provide just this. Think carefully though, as some schemes could backfire.

Love/Affection: Put a little bit of sparkle back into your private life. You may have been working so hard lately that you didn't notice the fire going out.

532 – BEETLE HEART LIGHTNING

General Situation: Don't just sit about day-dreaming of what might be, get up and do something positive. Once you've taken the plunge you'll be surprised just how much you can achieve in a short space of time.

Finance/Business: Provided that you are prepared to work hard and don't give in when the going gets a little tough, your financial position will improve beyond all recognition.

Love/Affection: You and your partner are in for a busy time when you'll be called upon to make snap decisions. This will have a very positive effect upon your relationship and you will both benefit in one way or another.

531 – BEETLE HEART SNAIL

General Situation: Others seem to be holding you back, especially your family. You will find this particularly irritating but if you take time to think about it they could be right. Ease up a bit, if you carry on overdoing things your health could suffer.

Finance/Business: Financially you really are in limbo at present. You have the drive and determination to succeed but don't seem to be able to find the right direction in which to channel it. Don't make any hurried decisions.

Love/Affection: Have a really good look at your relationship before making any plans for the future. Your partner may not be thinking along the same lines as you and should be given time to think things over. Be patient.

526 – BEETLE STORK FRUIT-TREE

General Situation: Now is the time to branch out and try something new. You've had the idea planned out in your mind for some months and it will only take a little application on your part to set things rolling.

Finance/Business: Promotion or a new role in your working life is indicated. This will be a busy period with new projects to be set up and fresh targets to aim for. An increase in income is likely.

Love/Affection: You really can't buy someone's affections – so don't try. Just be yourself and resist the temptation to turn someone's head with expensive presents.

525 – BEETLE STORK GOBLET

General Situation: Relax and enjoy yourself. Plan ahead for both leisure and work.

Finance/Business: If you're looking for something to invest in – anything to do with the catering trade looks promising. And if you only have a little cash, why not put down a crate or two of wine?

Love/Affection: A wonderful time for lovers whether married or single. Life will be one long round of pleasure with plenty to celebrate and some pleasant discoveries to make.

524 – BEETLE STORK KEY

General Situation: Come on, stir yourself. There's lots to be done and much to be gained. Forget your problems, you must move with the times and try something new for a change.

Finance/Business: If you've had some new ideas lately which could benefit not only you but your employer, make them known as soon as possible. This could be just the opportunity you've been waiting for.

Love/Affection: Harmonious would be the best way to describe your private life these days. Not only are you feeling happy and content but your partner feels the same way too.

523 – BEETLE STORK LADDER

General Situation: Life is what you make of it and your chance to make a dream come true is coming soon. Be ready to act and don't allow minor obstacles to put you off course.

Finance/Business: If you're tired of working for someone else this could be your chance to go it alone, but be prepared to work long hours to get the scheme off the ground.

Love/Affection: How about combining business with pleasure? You and your partner make a good team and neither of you are afraid of hard work. You've both always dreamed of setting up on your own – think about it.

522 – BEETLE STORK LIGHTNING

General Situation: A new idea or scheme which you have decided to pursue is not something which will be quickly achieved. It will require a great deal of thought and determination if this goal is to be achieved. An interesting time ahead.

Finance/Business: A new venture, possibly your own brain-child, is now viable but make sure that you have done your homework properly and haven't tried to cut corners. Don't sign any contracts or enter into any agreements hastily – read the small print with care. A break with tradition, however, could be to your advantage.

Love/Affection: A new romance or friendship seems likely to blossom very quickly, but don't do something foolish which you may regret later. Also don't become so infatuated that you forget all your other friends and interests. Get to know the person better before you make any long-term decisions.

521 – BEETLE STORK SNAIL

General Situation: You really must pay more attention to your health, even a little exercise is better than none at all. A few early nights wouldn't go amiss either if you want to be in peak condition to put all your new plans and ideas into action soon.

Finance/Business: Prosperity for you is just around the corner. Keep your ears and eyes open and be prepared to act. It would be a shame to miss a heaven-sent opportunity because you were caught napping at the crucial moment.

Love/Affection: You and your partner would both benefit from a few quiet nights at home just watching the television, reading a book or just generally relaxing. That candle won't burn at both ends for ever!

516 – BEETLE SUN FRUIT-TREE

General Situation: There really isn't any situation that you couldn't get the better of and come out on top. You will be full of energy and the desire to get things done will be very much in evidence.

Finance/Business: How can you possibly fail? It's almost as if you had the Midas touch as everything you become involved in pays off very handsome dividends. Even the odd silly gamble turns out to be a winner – but don't let it all go to your head.

Love/Affection: You may be feeling on top of a wave but is your partner? Make sure that you share your success and try not to be too full of yourself. A little more humility wouldn't go amiss.

515 – BEETLE SUN GOBLET

General Situation: Make hay while the sun shines and enjoy the fruits of your labours. Your devotion to duty has brought you success and you should share it with family and friends by celebrating a little.

Finance/Business: Don't allow very persuasive sales talk to turn your head. Keep your mind on your own personal goals and look extremely carefully at any offers you may be made that seem too good to be true – there's sure to be a catch somewhere.

Love/Affection: This will be a wonderful, happy time for lovers of all ages. However, don't be tempted to hide yourselves away – get out and about more and above all enjoy yourselves.

514 – BEETLE SUN KEY

General Situation: There will be a number of important opportunities coming your way – but you must look out for them. Talk over your future plans and ambitions with someone whose opinion you value but, above all, be ready to act.

Finance/Business: Opportunity is soon going to knock so make sure that it's you who opens the door to financial advancement. This could be the answer to all your problems. Act now!

Love/Affection: The scene is set for you to have a very happy and loving time provided that you take the initiative and don't hang back. For single people with marriage in mind there couldn't be a better time to pop the question and plan your future together.

513 – BEETLE SUN LADDER

General Situation: However wild and ambitious your ideas may seem, you couldn't ask for a better time to put them to the test. At the moment your life can be what you want to make of it.

Finance/Business: Before you forge ahead with some new scheme which will take all your time, energy and, perhaps, a lot of your hard-earned capital, just make sure that all the preliminary paper work is in order. For instance – are you properly insured?

Love/Affection: There's more to you than meets the eye and your partner will be surprised and delighted with some plans you've been making for you both.

512 – BEETLE SUN LIGHTNING

General Situation: However determined you may be to get a job done as quickly as possible, do be careful! Especially with machinery. Accidents happen so quickly so don't get careless.

Finance/Business: Try not to get too carried away, keep your financial transactions within a limit which you can afford. The temptation to overspend will be very strong. Resist it.

Love/Affection: Try not to upset matters by being selfish and getting so wrapped up in your own thoughts that you don't consider others. This could quite easily cause arguments and displays of temper from your partner.

511 – BEETLE SUN SNAIL

General Situation: Healthwise you will be feeling much fitter and more active than you have done for some time. However, use this new-found vitality carefully or it may not last.

Finance/Business: Your business outlook is first-class and your future prospects also look good. Don't go and spoil things by trying to cut corners or by making thoughtless errors of judgement.

Love/Affection: Don't go rushing into things or making any commitments which you might later regret. You've got plenty of time to think matters over and make sure that any decisions you make will be the right ones.

466 – HORSESHOE CROSSROADS FRUIT-TREE

General Situation: Any plans that you are making for home improvements or indeed a change of house should turn out well.

However, you may experience some preliminary setbacks. Don't let these put you off.

Finance/Business: This is a good time for taking some small financial risks but they must be small. Any scheme which could involve considerable financial outlay or perhaps even a second mortgage would not be advisable at present.

Love/Affection: You are in for a surprise and a very pleasant one at that. Your partner has been planning this treat for some time so make sure that you show your appreciation.

465 – HORSESHOE CROSSROADS GOBLET

General Situation: You will receive an invitation from a person you have only recently met. It will be to a social function of some kind, a party maybe. Go – it will really be an eye-opener.

Finance/Business: While it can be very pleasant to spend money on wining and dining occasionally, this is becoming rather a habit with you. Take a little more care of the pennies as you will need them to invest in something special very soon.

Love/Affection: For married couples, this will be a very happy period of your lives with plenty to do and plenty to celebrate. Single people could well meet someone over a casual drink who will become very important in their lives.

464 – HORSESHOE CROSSROADS KEY

General Situation: By a sheer stroke of good luck you will find yourself on the receiving end of an extremely good offer. This may cause friends to be jealous but it will solve a lot of your worries in one go.

Finance/Business: You will soon be able to purchase something which you have your heart set on and which you have been saving up for over the last few years. This extra money will come from a lottery, a small pools win or maybe even a lucky bet on the horses.

Love/Affection: You and your partner will be able to settle your differences at long last. Your relationship will become stronger and more permanent.

463 – HORSESHOE CROSSROADS LADDER

General Situation: Luck is with you at the moment and so are good health and ample energy. Now is the time to make any decisions which could prove to be turning points in your life. Depending on how you decide to do things, it could also see you climbing the ladder of success. Turn a chance event into an advantage.

Finance/Business: If you ever wanted to take a chance and hesitated before – don't hesitate now, gambles or risks are sure to pay off. A surprise promotion or increase of funds is also indicated.

Love/Affection: Everything in the garden is rosy – happiness, laughter and affection abound. For single people now is a good time to think about settling down and making plans for the future.

462 – HORSESHOE CROSSROADS LIGHTNING

General Situation: Something totally unforseen and unplanned for will spoil the arrangements which you have been making. Let it – you will soon realize that it was a blessing in disguise.

Finance/Business: Keep your eyes open for a member of a rival company or concern who could well be practising a little industrial espionage. It could be very annoying to find that your plans had been copied.

Love/Affection: Stop being so moody and brooding about an episode which, if not forgotten, has been forgiven. Shake yourself out of this depression and do something positive and decisive.

461 – HORSESHOE CROSSROADS SNAIL

General Situation: Patience is a virtue and one which you seem to be lacking. Don't fret so much about delays and hold-ups – they can work for you as well as against.

Finance/Business: If you have money which can be tied up for several years in a long-term investment without leaving you short of working capital then go ahead and invest. Short-term schemes, however, do not look so promising.

Love/Affection: 'Give and take' in a relationship is what keeps it going but you seem to have been taking more than your fair share. It is time to reverse this situation.

456 – HORSESHOE CAT FRUIT-TREE

General Situation: Anything which you chose to get involved in will prosper and will benefit both you and your family. A chance to try something completely new will also be to your advantage.

Finance/Business: The way things are going the Jones' will have to keep up with you. At long last you'll be able to afford to make some improvements to your home which will greatly increase its value.

Love/Affection: Stay just as you are – that's just how your partner and friends like you and why you're so happy and contented.

455 – HORSESHOE CAT GOBLET

General Situation: Now that you seem to have made the grade and all your interests are thriving you deserve a treat. So do your family who have stood by you in the past. Throw a party to say thank you or take them all out for a meal.

Finance/Business: It's not generally a good idea to invest in the entertainment industry but it could prove very profitable for you. You might even consider taking over a country pub with your family, or even running a little bistro in town.

Love/Affection: Some of that little windfall you have just received – or soon will – should be spent on your partner. You both deserve a night out.

454 – HORSESHOE CAT KEY

General Situation: A secret worry which you have been keeping from your family for some time will soon be solved by a stroke of good luck. Then you can be your old cheerful self again.

Finance/Business: Now is the time to improve your financial situation by expanding your business interests and branching out into something new. The onus is on you to take the initiative.

Love/Affection: If family worries and responsibilities have been weighing rather heavily on you, try to make time in your busy day when you and your partner can be alone together. You both need some time off to relax.

453 – HORSESHOE CAT LADDER

General Situation: The time is right to turn your hopes into realities. Move with the times and channel all that nervous energy of yours into reaching your goal. Don't wait for family approval – just go ahead.

Finance/Business: Your family and home will be the main drain on your finances in the coming months. However, whether you decide on a move of home, building an extension or just redecorating a room it will be money well spent which will bring pleasure to you all.

Love/Affection: If you've been letting yourself go a little, now is the time to smarten yourself up. Don't allow familiarity to breed contempt, your partner is sure to appreciate the effort.

452 – HORSESHOE CAT LIGHTNING

General Situation: Don't go bringing the wrath of your entire family down about your ears just because you've acted on the spur of the moment and made a foolish mistake. Discuss plans first and then everyone will stay happy.

Finance/Business: Don't risk all the capital that you've worked so hard to build up on a rush business deal or an impulse buy. You should be sure that you are in possession of all the facts and have had plenty of time for thought before you act.

Love/Affection: You should try to be a little more demonstrative towards your partner if you want to keep in their good books. A little present to show your appreciation might help to show that they're not taken too much for granted.

451 – HORSESHOE CAT SNAIL

General Situation: It's about time you took a break and gave yourself some time to think. A few days at home doing nothing would soon see you refreshed and raring to go again.

Finance/Business: Business matters should be thought over, carefully planned and then executed and not entered into on the spur of the moment without prior consideration. This can only lead you into problems.

Love/Affection: It wouldn't hurt to show your partner a little more affection or at least consideration. Don't overdo it, though, or they may think you're up to something.

446 – HORSESHOE KNIFE FRUIT-TREE

General Situation: Check out that your house and its contents are adequately insured. Also make sure that all your doors and windows are properly secured because there's a lot of petty theft about and you don't want to fall victim to it.

Finance/Business: Keep the details of your financial position to yourself. There are people around who are dishonest and may try to relieve you of some of your hard-earned money if they can get the chance.

Love/Affection: Is there a rival for your partner's affections? Do nothing for the moment as it may be quite harmless but be prepared to act should it be necessary.

445 – HORSESHOE KNIFE GOBLET

General Situation: Your outlook for the future seems to be set for success but don't go counting your chickens too soon, this is not yet the time for reckless spending. What could your friends be keeping from you?

Finance/Business: Business and pleasure really do not mix, especially at the moment – you should know this by now. They really must be kept separate if you want your plans to succeed.

Love/Affection: All these arguments must stop, these petty little jealousies and grumbles are not worth the fuss. No relationship is perfect and the sooner you realize it the sooner you will be able to put things on an even keel again.

444 – HORSESHOE KNIFE KEY

General Situation: You may not appreciate it now but that opportunity you missed was a blessing in disguise. It would have been a very risky venture. However, don't despair as a second chance is coming which will be very much more in your line.

Finance/Business: Watch out for friction at work between two of your workmates. Do your best to patch things up between them before their bickering upsets some of your well laid plans.

Love/Affection: The only good thing about arguments is making up afterwards. If you want to avoid arguments altogether try to be a little more open with your partner and explain to them what you have been planning.

443 – HORSESHOE KNIFE LADDER

General Situation: Generally things look very promising for you but it would not be a good idea to take too many risks or you could come unstuck. A little careful forward planning will help.

Finance/Business: A most unlikely person, one you never dreamed was on your side, will single you out for higher things. Make the most of this golden opportunity.

Love/Affection: You really must try to be a little more tolerant about your partner's shortcomings. Stop criticizing and be a little more helpful instead, it might make a difference.

442 – HORSESHOE KNIFE LIGHTNING

General Situation: If you wish to avoid annoying delays and setbacks try to curb your enthusiasm a little. Put those good ideas into action one step at a time after much careful thought and consideration. More haste – less speed!

Finance/Business: Your financial and business prospects look excellent. Don't go spoiling matters through over-hastiness or cutting corners.

Love/Affection: You may be feeling rather jealous because your partner seems to have so many commitments and interests which you don't share. Stop feeling so resentful and instead find something you can do together.

441 – HORSESHOE KNIFE SNAIL

General Situation: Problems concerning the care of an elderly relative will seem to be never-ending. Try not to let this become a drain on your own health and strength. Whenever you find you have some spare time use it to do something you want to do for a change.

Finance/Business: You have few money worries and problems at the moment. However, this doesn't mean that you can afford to go taking risks. Always think matters over carefully before you decide to take action.

Love/Affection: If your emotional life seems to have become a little stale and boring it could well be your own fault. Give it a stir and try something new.

436 – HORSESHOE HEART FRUIT-TREE

General Situation: This is a tremendous combination of symbols. Whatever you decide to do will be successful and you really can't go wrong. Enjoy it while it lasts.

Finance/Business: Now is the time to splash out and invest in a hobby or on some personal indulgence which you are unable to resist. Any money spent on the home and family will prove to be a good investment.

Love/Affection: This is your time when everything will be going for you. Make the most of it and really savour every moment.

435 – HORSESHOE HEART GOBLET

General Situation: This is a period with plenty to do and much to celebrate. Activities with friends or family are indicated.

Finance/Business: It's odd how things tend to snowball and this is just what's about to happen to you. Something which started off as a gamble will suddenly catch on and grow at an alarming speed.

Love/Affection: Try to forget about money for a while because this is a time for love and togetherness. The rat race will still be there waiting for you, but at the moment your relationship is more important.

434 – HORSESHOE HEART KEY

General Situation: By a sheer stroke of good luck you will get the opportunity to do something you've always dreamed of. Do it well and who knows where it could lead you.

Finance/Business: Long term plans will meet with the approval of a friend who has the right kind of influence to help promote them. This is an almost heaven-sent opportunity for you to break into new fields of activity.

Love/Affection: Your private life just couldn't be better, or could it? If you have plans or proposals to put to your partner concerning your future, now is the time to do it.

433 – HORSESHOE HEART LADDER

General Situation: By your own sheer hard work you will make great strides towards a personal goal. This will be a very rewarding experience although not necessarily in a momentary sense.

Finance/Business: The success of an important and, in the opinion of some people, rather an ambitious project is almost certainly assured. However, you must double-check that you have done your sums properly before embarking upon it.

Love/Affection: If your partner has had their heart set upon something which would undoubtedly give them great pleasure why not try to get it for them as a surprise. But only if it's financially possible.

432 – HORSESHOE HEART LIGHTNING

General Situation: Sudden good fortune from a most unexpected quarter will mean that you have to change some of your plans slightly. Make sure that your family understand what you're trying to do or friction could result.

Finance/Business: Although generally not a good idea, you could make an exception this time and have a little flutter on the horses especially on one named after a member of your family. But don't make it a habit.

Love/Affection: An impulsive action on your part could bring a little sparkle back into your life. It will bring enjoyment to you and your partner and a few surprises too.

431 – HORSESHOE HEART SNAIL

General Situation: Luck seems to be smiling on you and the Midas touch will be much in evidence in everything you do. Matters of the heart are also well aspected and you will be surrounded by love and affection. However, watch your health! Don't take liberties and burn the candle at both ends. Good luck and love won't do you much good if you're feeling too tired to enjoy them.

Finance/Business: Provided that you avoid making silly and hurried decisions, nothing much can go wrong at present. Not only will your plans be successful but you have the backing and help of colleagues as well. It may even be worth taking a business risk provided that you calculate the odds carefully at first.

Love/Affection: A happy, loving time with your family. Between you and your partner, love will be given as well as received just when you were thinking things had gone a little flat. Much laughter and happiness.

426 – HORSESHOE STORK FRUIT-TREE

General Situation: You will shortly be entering into a very creative phase in your life when you should promote any new ideas you may have, however revolutionary they may seem. Some are sure to bear fruit.

Finance/Business: Your main problem during the coming period will be finding the time to benefit from some of the money you'll be so busy earning. You'll also have the pleasure of saying that 'it's all my own work'.

Love/Affection: You and your partner should pool your resources. Your combined talents, if channelled in the right direction, make a formidable union.

425 – HORSESHOE STORK GOBLET

General Situation: If you haven't got anything in particular to celebrate then you must just sit down and invent something. This is no time for staying at home.

Finance/Business: Don't give up now and throw the towel in if some venture isn't going quite to plan. Re-think the situation and perhaps after one or two minor modifications you'll be ready to go. A breakthrough is coming.

Love/Affection: All in all this will be a hectic but enjoyable time.

424 – HORSESHOE STORK KEY

General Situation: You are in for a run of good luck which is long overdue.

Finance/Business: Before taking advantage of a very generous offer, it would be sensible to study all the implications. If you doubt your own business sense, then seek expert advice.

Love/Affection: This time you're on your own and your partner can't help you except by being a good listener as and when you need one. Take advantage of this.

423 – HORSESHOE STORK LADDER

General Situation: Good luck together with creative ability will enable you to achieve a special ambition. Careful planning is the key as without this problems could occur.

Finance/Business: In order to build up some capital, it may be necessary to take the odd calculated risk or two. Your rather tenuous plans need a little more thought before they can be considered viable.

Love/Affection: You two really do need some sort of target or ambition to channel your energies into, instead of just sitting around feeling bored. Put your heads together and see what you can come up with.

422 – HORSESHOE STORK LIGHTNING

General Situation: This is a creative time when you will be required to work under pressure. Enter into things wholeheartedly as there can be no half measures. You may not gain financially from this but your reputation will certainly be enhanced.

Finance/Business: Try not to make your 'ambitious streak' quite so obvious. There is someone in a senior position who may be worried for his own job and who may resort to a few cunning tricks to make sure that you remain where you are.

Love/Affection: Although you may find a colleague of the opposite sex extremely attractive, this should stay a case of worship from afar. Don't do anything precipitous or you might regret it.

421 – HORSESHOE STORK SNAIL

General Situation: You must take more care of yourself. Go to bed early for a change. You can't expect peak performance when you neglect yourself.

Finance/Business: Don't allow family pressure to coerce you into buying something rather expensive for the home on the spur of the moment. If you take time to shop around you'll be surprised how much prices differ from shop to shop.

Love/Affection: Spend some time alone with your partner and use this time to formulate a few long-term plans.

416 – HORSESHOE SUN FRUIT-TREE

General Situation: Your outlook for the future just couldn't be better. Dreams should soon become realities and you should be feeling very pleased with yourself. You will be feeling in peak condition and raring to go. Enjoy yourself.

Finance/Business: This will be a time of plenty, when not only will you be able to make ends meet without a struggle but you will also have some surplus cash to spend on the home or other interests. Promotion at work is indicated.

Love/Affection: Keep an eye on any joint accounts as your partner may have been overspending in an attempt to keep up with the Jones's. It would be a good idea to review your financial position together so that you both know how much you can afford to spend on luxuries.

415 – HORSESHOE SUN GOBLET

General Situation: Through a stroke of good fortune a rather risky scheme will actually come off.

Finance/Business: A rather interesting business proposition could be put to you over a meal. However, find out a little more about it before making any commitment – the wine may have gone to your head.

Love/Affection: It's no good saying that you never meet anyone new when you don't go anywhere. Get out and about a bit more or even throw a party of your own. Do something positive.

414 – HORSESHOE SUN KEY

General Situation: Don't allow your family and friends to ride rough-shod over you. Be more assertive and make them do what you want just for once. Don't become a 'yes' man or woman just for the sake of a little peace and quiet.

Finance/Business: It will be necessary to delegate more in order to get through your increasingly heavy workload. This will also enable you to gain a little more time to spend on a rather ambitious and complicated venture of your own.

Love/Affection: A change of partner is indicated which will be relatively easy to accomplish for single people. Think matters over with great care before arriving at any decision.

413 – HORSESHOE SUN LADDER

General Situation: Lady Luck has decided to smile on you so you will have little trouble getting whatever you want no matter how ambitious it may seem. Make the most of your opportunities and above all enjoy your success.

Finance/Business: What a success story yours will be as long as you keep your head and remain firmly in control of the situation. Take the plunge and go all out for success – you're sure to reach the top.

Love/Affection: You and your partner make a formidable team and provided that you pull together you will achieve a great deal.

412 – HORSESHOE SUN LIGHTNING

General Situation: An impulsive action could well start a whole new way of life for you and it will set into motion a chain of events that you had not bargained for. Go ahead – leap before you look for a change.

Finance/Business: If you are ambitious and want to get on in life then this could be the right time to consider changing your career. Seek a position with more responsibility and greater scope for advancement.

Love/Affection: Whatever it was you did to make your partner so indignant you had better hurry up and make amends somehow.

The longer you leave it the harder it will be to restore peace and harmony to your relationship.

411 – HORSESHOE SUN SNAIL

General Situation: You've had a busy time lately and have much to be thankful for. Allow yourself a little more time to relax and count your blessings. Don't forget to thank those who gave you a helping hand.

Finance/Business: Use this slack period to catch up on all your paper-work, but be careful what you write, especially if filling in tax forms or legal documents. You must make things quite clear or misunderstandings will occur.

Love/Affection: You both deserve a holiday so take a break from that hectic life of yours when you seem to be constantly working against time to get things done. A little time together with nothing to do would be a pleasant change.

366 – BOAT CROSSROADS FRUIT-TREE

General Situation: Don't be surprised if you are suddenly required to pack your bags and rush off somewhere. You will find that this will result in some kind of personal gain although it may not be just money.

Finance/Business: The outcome of a report at work will really put the cat amongst the pigeons and will leave one or two people with rather red faces – make sure that you are not one of them. Auditors can uncover all sorts of errors.

Love/Affection: It's about time you made a few new friends in your neighbourhood. Someone you will meet at a social function will have a great influence on your plans for the future.

365 – BOAT CROSSROADS GOBLET

General Situation: A letter is coming which will contain some rather unexpected news. You will have to revise a few plans and perhaps cancel one or two engagements in order to gain time to consider the matter.

Finance/Business: A business contact which you made some time ago, and never got around to following up, will be re-established through an unexpected telephone call. Don't lose touch this time or you will miss an important lead.

Love/Affection: Oh dear! Someone from your dark and murky past is about to make an unexpected re-appearance. Watch out for quarrels and jealousy.

364 – BOAT CROSSROADS KEY

General Situation: During the coming period you will receive many interesting and varied offers and you will find it hard to decide which one to follow up. You could even get the chance to travel so make sure that your passport is up-to-date.

Finance/Business: Keep an eye on strangers who you feel are somehow rather suspicious, particularly if you are going away for any period of time and will be leaving your property unattended. Double check that all doors and windows are safely secured.

Love/Affection: Watch out for someone who has recently joined your circle of friends. They may see you as the answer to all their problems and could spring one or two nasty surprises.

363 – BOAT CROSSROADS LADDER

General Situation: If you are at all ambitious follow up a surprise opportunity which will come your way – it could lead to bigger things and at the very least will be most enjoyable.

Finance/Business: Now is the time to check up on what business rivals are up to – you could be in for a bit of a shock. Get out and about more and do some research in the field if you want to stay abreast of current trends.

Love/Affection: Nothing ventured – nothing gained. Try to put matters right between you and your partner with a telephone call or even a little present. You have reached a crossroads in your relationship and it's up to you to decide which path you want to take.

362 – BOAT CROSSROADS LIGHTNING

General Situation: This is a time for action and you should get on the move. Why not pay a surprise visit to some friends or relatives that you haven't seen for some time. Failing that there must be some letters you should have written or telephone calls you should have made.

Finance/Business: Don't allow an increase in your workload to make you careless. You must not be tempted to rush a job and turn out a second-rate performance. Be prepared for a letter bearing some unexpected news.

Love/Affection: Don't be too quick off the mark to blame your partner if one or two things start to go wrong. It could be your fault. You must be more tolerant and patient.

361 – BOAT CROSSROADS SNAIL

General Situation: If you are planning any journeys, no matter how short, be prepared for hold-ups and delays. In fact it would be a good idea to set off a little earlier than necessary just in case.

Finance/Business: This is not a good time to go taking any risks either business-wise or with your own money. You would be better advised to mark time for a while until the economic situation improves. Instead, use this time to formulate new plans which can be implemented later.

Love/Affection: Try not to do anything foolish in front of strangers or your partner may be embarrassed and annoyed by your behaviour. Think before you act.

356 – BOAT CAT FRUIT-TREE

General Situation: A piece of information that you will receive from a close relative or in-law will be of considerable interest to you. If you act wisely you should be able to benefit from it.

Finance/Business: Make a very careful check of your finances as you might find that you have been overcharged for something you have recently purchased. Also make sure that an important letter hasn't gone unnoticed or unanswered. It could save you money.

Love/Affection: Day-dreaming about what might be is all very well in its place but your constant head in the clouds attitude could be very irritating for your partner. If you've been fantasizing over a holiday abroad or a better house, do something positive about it for a change.

355 – BOAT CAT GOBLET

General Situation: There couldn't be a better time to enjoy yourself than now. But don't just do it alone, make sure that you include your family too. Plan a get-together, a weekend away or even a night out at the cinema or a local restaurant – you'll all be sure to have a good time.

Finance/Business: Good news is on the way that will benefit both you and your family financially and socially. Something which you had previously thought impossible can now be done with relative ease.

Love/Affection: Be prepared – your social life is about to go into top gear. Lots of new and exciting people to meet and fun things to do. Foreign travel is also indicated.

354 – BOAT CAT KEY

General Situation: Life really can be what you decide to make of it as you have everything going for you just now – opportunities, lucky chances, family backing and approval. You have a free hand so play it carefully and you should not go wrong.

Finance/Business: Your business outlook for the coming period seems excellent. However, in order to take full advantage of chances that will arise you must be prepared to make a sacrifice of some kind which could prove a difficult decision for you.

Love/Affection: Any change in your partner, however slight, whether in attitude or in appearance, should not go unnoticed by you. Talk about it as there is a definite reason for this change.

353 – BOAT CAT LADDER

General Situation: If you are ambitious, opportunity won't come looking for you at home. You must be prepared to get out and about and make yourself known to people. The potential is there if only you use it.

Finance/Business: It might be a good idea to see if your family would be willing to back you financially in a new project that you want to get off the ground. Don't be too proud to ask.

Love/Affection: Your family will be very much involved in your personal affairs one way or another over this coming period. But remember that there are some things that are best kept to yourself.

352 – BOAT CAT LIGHTNING

General Situation: If you make any spur-of-the-moment plans for a holiday or an outing you could find yourself in hot water with those around you who may have different ideas. Talk things over with them.

Finance/Business: If a relative or in-law comes to you with a request for some kind of financial assistance you should treat this matter with great care. A quixotic gesture on your part could be the start of something you will later regret.

Love/Affection: Do something impulsive. Take your partner completely by surprise with an un-birthday present or have a night out to celebrate the cat's birthday. Anything will do so long as it is out of the ordinary.

351 – BOAT CAT SNAIL

General Situation: A break in the sun could be just what you need to help you relax and regain some of your energy. Get away from your home and family if only for a few days to give yourself time to think. If you really can't get away then take the phone off the hook and try to forget about everything for a while.

Finance/Business: Take great care if you have to sign any legal documents, especially if they involve your house or personal possessions. If there is something which you don't understand you must make it your business to find out. And if there is anything which you don't like the look of, then ask for extra time to mull things over. Avoid hurried decisions!

Love/Affection: Try not to make any hasty plans where your private life is concerned. Think matters over very carefully and make sure that you are in full possession of all the facts before reaching a decision.

346 – BOAT KNIFE FRUIT-TREE

General Situation: It would be advisable to double-check any plans you have made through a third-party – especially where travel arrangements are concerned. A telephone call now could save you a lot of trouble and embarrassment later on.

Finance/Business: Avoid delegating responsibilities which are really yours as other people may not be quite so conscientious as you. There is a colleague who would be only too glad to see you make a mistake.

Love/Affection: Make sure that any messages or notes you may leave for your partner are crystal clear or you may return to find yourself in their bad books. A little more thoughtfulness on your part could avoid unnecessary arguments.

345 – BOAT KNIFE GOBLET

General Situation: A surprise invitation to party or celebration may not be as innocuous as it first seems. If you decide to accept you must remember to keep your wits about you or you may be deceived.

Finance/Business: Pay careful attention to the menu when dining out with a business associate or client. Stick to what you know especially if ordering foreign food.

Love/Affection: If communications between you and your partner seem to have broken down slightly and have become rather monosyllabic, why not have a quiet meal out and patch things up. You can't solve a problem until you have talked things over and found the cause.

344 – BOAT KNIFE KEY

General Situation: You should think very carefully before embarking on any new undertaking, especially if it appears to be a heaven-sent opportunity to solve a few personal problems. It is far easier to fail than to succeed, so don't leave anything to chance.

Finance/Business: Now would be a very good time to consider a change of job, especially if you have been working for a very politically-structured organization. Don't do anything precipitous but be on the look-out for an opening elsewhere.

Love/Affection: Holiday romances are all very well and can be great fun if you don't allow yourself to become too involved. Just as you might put on an act away from home to impress another, so can someone else. Don't be made to look a fool.

343 – BOAT KNIFE LADDER

General Situation: Play things very close to your chest, especially where your personal ambitions are concerned. Once you let another into your confidence you run the risk of having your plans spoilt.

Finance/Business: When taking a gamble, especially with your own money, make sure that you really can afford to lose. New projects can cost a great deal of money to set up so don't be in too much of a hurry to invest and don't believe everything you're told. Check things out for yourself first.

Love/Affection: In a personal relationship you must be prepared to make your feelings known even if this does spark off arguments and quarrels. Try not to be timid, you must clear the air to find out if what exists between you is really worth having or whether your relationship has just become a habit.

342 – BOAT KNIFE LIGHTNING

General Situation: As the result of a letter or telephone call, it will soon be necessary for you to make a journey. You will probably find this irritating but the journey is vital.

Finance/Business: Due to problems with business communications, it may be necessary for you to make a number of short journeys. Be prepared to meet unwelcome people on your travels.

Love/Affection: Avoid misleading someone. Make sure that you really know what you want. It would be thoughtless and unfeeling to let them down at the last moment because you change your mind.

341 – BOAT KNIFE SNAIL

General Situation: You must try to slow your pace if you don't want your health to suffer from overwork. Try to plan your workload so that you don't have to make more journeys than necessary. Don't be tricked into doing something which you really think is beyond your capabilities.

Finance/Business: This is a time to be like the ostrich and keep your head well down – if not actually buried. Avoid the temptation to invest money, however small an amount, even if the scheme looks like a winner.

Love/Affection: Try not to let your restlessness irritate your partner. This period will soon pass and you should concentrate on relaxing together and generally taking things a little easier.

336 – BOAT HEART FRUIT-TREE

General Situation: Now could be a good time to take a sentimental journey and visit old friends and old places. You might even learn something about yourself.

Finance/Business: If you or your firm have any money tied up in foreign investments it would be a good idea to keep a close eye on the political situations of the countries in question. Be prepared to either withdraw or invest quickly, once you have assessed the situation.

Love/Affection: If you want to create a good impression with your partner or a loved one, now is the time to spend a little money on them as a show of your appreciation.

335 – BOAT HEART GOBLET

General Situation: It should now be possible for you to achieve something which you had hitherto thought impossible. Someone influential should be instrumental in this. Watch the post.

Finance/Business: A rather successful business venture in which you are involved will give you much cause to celebrate. But don't take all the glory for yourself.

Love/Affection: Avoid getting too involved in your own triumphs and achievements so that you forget to include your partner in your success.

334 – BOAT HEART KEY

General Situation: An opportunity could arise which might bring a solution to a problem which has been worrying you. This opportunity might be revealed after receiving a letter. A change of home is also a possibility. This is something you have wanted for some time.

Finance/Business: A busy time ahead with many letters to be written and telephone calls to be made. An opening could arise which will give you the opportunity to combine both business and pleasure. It could even be a change of job.

Love/Affection: A trip to see relatives who live some distance away and the chance to sort out family problems face-to-face will probably result from a message. Don't keep old misunderstandings to yourself. Air your grievances as you may have the wrong impression.

333 – BOAT HEART LADDER

General Situation: This is a good time to visit family or friends who live abroad. Apart from enjoying yourself, it might give you some insight into the way other people tackle various problems. And this might help you at a later date.

Finance/Business: Although this could be a very eventful period for you with new projects to be launched, try not to neglect your loved ones. If you have to stay away from home for any length of time, remember to keep in touch.

Love/Affection: It is quite possible that on your travels you will make an important new friendship. This would be worth cultivating and could be of help to you in the future.

332 – BOAT HEART LIGHTNING

General Situation: Some information you will receive about a friend should be taken with a pinch of salt. Messages sometimes have a habit of getting distorted and it would be a shame to spoil a good friendship through a misunderstanding.

Finance/Business: Should you have to be absent from work or home for a period, make sure that you have appointed a friend or member of your family to delegate for you. An important letter or telephone call may require immediate action.

Love/Affection: You must remember to keep your partner up to date with any plans you are making, especially if they involve travel. You may be regarded with suspicion if you go rushing off somewhere without a word of warning.

331 – BOAT HEART SNAIL

General Situation: If you are feeling tired and want a day or two to relax, don't let friends talk you into doing something strenuous.

Finance/Business: Don't allow personal feelings to cloud a financial decision you will have to make. Study all the facts very carefully and pay attention to small print.

Love/Affection: Unavoidable delays may prevent you from being on time when meeting your partner for a special occasion. Try to get a message through somehow.

326 – BOAT STORK FRUIT-TREE

General Situation: A new baby coming into your family will be prosperous and much travelled in later life. An idea of your own which you are trying to promote could well prove to be a money-spinner abroad. Put pen to paper and make enquiries about overseas outlets.

Finance/Business: In order to solve financial problems it might be necessary to go back to square one and do some rethinking. New ideas or a new approach are necessary if you want to get out of (and stay out of) the red.

Love/Affection: If you and your partner want to keep your relationship happy and fulfilling then avoid arguments over money at all costs. By all means discuss financial matters but always on a friendly basis – if you don't then you could find yourselves parting company.

325 – BOAT STORK GOBLET

General Situation: Life for you is going to be busy and full of fun. However, don't go discussing your ideas and future intentions with strangers. No matter how good the company and how chatty you are feeling, keep your own business very much to yourself. Careless talk could cost you your ideas.

Finance/Business: The best time for you to get over new ideas and proposals would be at a business luncheon or over drinks after work with either your boss, your colleagues or an important client. It could provide just the opportunity you have been waiting for.

Love/Affection: Your partner could well try to sweet-talk you into something. Go along with their plan.

324 – BOAT STORK KEY

General Situation: The chance will arise to try something creative and completely outside your normal range of activities. Have a go – you could be pleasantly surprised by the outcome.

Finance/Business: Workwise it looks as if you will be in for a very busy and eventful time. New doors will be opening for you but it's up to you to make sure they stay open. You will only succeed through your own efforts. Foreign travel is also indicated.

Love/Affection: It seems likely that someone new will come into your life whom you will find both different and stimulating. This could be just the chance you have been waiting for.

323 – BOAT STORK LADDER

General Situation: Write a few letters or telephone around to see if you can find someone who would be interested in your ideas. You won't get anywhere if you don't try, so sell yourself more.

Finance/Business: If business seems a little slow in this country, then why not make enquiries to see if you might do better for yourself abroad. If you are ambitious then you should be prepared to go where the best prospects are.

Love/Affection: Your present relationship seems to have stagnated so it's up to you to decide whether to cut your losses or whether to try again. If you do opt for a second chance, then try to show a little more enthusiasm and be generally more demonstrative.

322 – BOAT STORK LIGHTNING

General Situation: Avoid writing letters or making telephone calls in anger. Try to find out what has gone wrong. You could discover that plans have not been properly explained to you and that once you are in the picture all will be well.

Finance/Business: This would be a good time to have all electrical appliances and communications equipment such as telephones and telexes at work checked out. Look out your service agreements and get this done swiftly. You may be quite shocked by the engineers' findings.

Love/Affection: You and your partner should start thinking very seriously about your plans for the future. However, before you embark on anything new, take sufficient time to talk things over and to view your ideas from all angles. Make some written notes if it helps.

321 – BOAT STORK SNAIL

General Situation: Any important decisions you have to make will keep for the time being. The most important thing to do is to restore yourself to peak condition, perhaps a general medical examination would set your mind at rest.

Finance/Business: It's a good time to visit the trade shows, seminars and meetings in your particular industry or field. Keep your eyes open for new approaches to old problems and bear these in mind for future reference. Don't be tempted to invest any money at the moment – look, learn but don't buy.

Love/Affection: Where your private life is concerned, your probable best course of action would be to stay at home with some good books to read or catch up on any outstanding correspondence. Don't do anything on impulse as your ideas are unlikely to come to anything at the moment.

316 – BOAT SUN FRUIT-TREE

General Situation: Good news from abroad could brighten up your life and could even be the reason for you having to do some travelling later in the year. Start saving up now.

Finance/Business: A complete reshuffle at work looks likely when all the dead wood will be pruned out quite savagely. However, there's no need for you to worry as this will leave the way clear for you to rise a little higher up the ladder. If you are offered the chance to invest in your firm then take it.

Love/Affection: A cheerful, happy, harmonious time ahead for you if you're married. And if you happen to be single then watch out as someone new and very special is about to enter your life.

315 – BOAT SUN GOBLET

General Situation: Try being a little more cheerful and personable – it could help in more ways than one.

Finance/Business: If you really want to succeed and get on in this world you must try to be more forceful and decisive. Stop wishing for the impossible and instead channel your energies into projects which are within your capabilities. Success can be yours if you could only be more realistic.

Love/Affection: Some good news that you and your partner will receive will spur you on to attempt something you have both been contemplating for some time now. This calls for a celebration.

314 – BOAT SUN KEY

General Situation: You probably have worries and problems. These won't solve themselves so you must seize every opportunity you can find to put matters right. This will probably be very time-consuming but once you have things back on an even keel again you'll be glad you bothered.

Finance/Business: Promotion and more responsibility will come your way very soon. This opportunity could also involve a great deal of travelling which you may not want. Think very carefully before reaching a decision as you won't be asked a second time.

Love/Affection: It may be necessary for you and your partner to be separated for a while should you decide to take a job away from home. Don't worry too much as you are sure to make a success of things and you'll be re-united very soon.

313 – BOAT SUN LADDER

General Situation: A journey which you make for pleasure will have a few pleasant surprises for you. You will return full of enthusiasm and with many new ideas you will want to put into action immediately.

Finance/Business: If you have been thinking of moving home and investigating in a bigger or better property then this could be the right time to make the move.

Love/Affection: If you and your partner have ever discussed going into business together and never got round to doing anything about it, then you should start rethinking again, right now. It could be the best move you are likely to make.

312 – BOAT SUN LIGHTNING

General Situation: Don't allow a misunderstanding between you and a friend to get out of proportion. Instead of sitting and brooding about it, go and see them immediately to put matters right.

Finance/Business: Take great care to avoid any accidents at work which could result from a lapse in concentration. Be especially careful if driving a firm's car or when travelling to or from a business appointment.

Love/Affection: This should be a very rewarding time for both you and your partner when there will be much to do and many arrangements to make. You should also derive tremendous pleasure from each other's company, when a greater harmony and understanding will develop.

311 – BOAT SUN SNAIL

General Situation: You seem to be filled with an almost overwhelming desire to travel but this may not be possible because of obstacles you will encounter which will prohibit your movements. You could be extremely glad later on that you remained.

Finance/Business: You may find that your telephone and postage bills are unusually high over the next few months but this is a necessary expenditure which will help you to pull off an ambitious venture that you have had in mind for some time. One word of warning though – make sure that you make yourself fully understood.

Love/Affection: Try not to be so full of yourself and your own importance that you don't take interest in your partner's ideas and plans. Pay them a little more attention, make sure that you listen to what they have to say and, above all – don't interrupt.

266 – SKULL CROSSROADS FRUIT-TREE

General Situation: If you have recently moved (or are about to) to a new locality then watch out for someone who appears over-friendly. Don't go telling them about your business or you could find them stirring up trouble for both you and your family.

Finance/Business: Financially, you could be faced with a decision you must make. Should you spend some money on the house you now live in or should you move to somewhere bigger and better, let your family help you to make up your mind.

Love/Affection: Don't allow an outsider to stir up trouble between you and your partner. They may have some unpleasant things to say, but try not to over-react to them. Think matters over and don't go making hasty moves.

265 – SKULL CROSSROADS GOBLET

General Situation: Gatecrashers at a party could cause trouble, and what was supposed to be a happy occasion for you and your friends could turn into chaos. Check your guest list very carefully and don't admit strangers.

Finance/Business: You could be in for some changes at work which you had least expected. An outsider, maybe an auditor or a new member of staff could create problems given half a chance. Watch out that your name doesn't appear on a redundancy list.

Love/Affection: Don't feel so safe and smug in your relationship as you do or you could be in for a bit of an eye-opener from a meddling neighbour. Pull your socks up and try to correct some of your worst faults.

264 – SKULL CROSSROADS KEY

General Situation: If you are at all worried about your health you would be well advised to see your GP and let him check things out for you – you are probably worrying yourself over nothing. Your family may be helpful and supportive but they are not qualified to make a diagnosis.

Finance/Business: An unexpected benefactor could arrive just in time to save you from a financially difficult situation. Learn from your mistakes and don't let yourself slide back into the same rut in another few months' time – you may not be so lucky again.

Love/Affection: Don't allow your family to meddle in your private affairs; what goes on between you and your partner is really none of their business. Ignore their attempts to influence you and follow your own feelings.

263 – SKULL CROSSROADS LADDER

General Situation: Don't allow the thought of failure to enter your mind if you embark upon something new. There's nothing you can't achieve when you really put your mind to it.

Finance/Business: If you really are hell-bent to try out something rather unheard of which you believe could change your lifestyle, then have a go. The choice is yours but don't allow other people with few ideas of their own to put you off.

Love/Affection: You are in for a very pleasant surprise which will leave you speechless for a while. Enjoy it while it lasts as it will be transitory and you will then have to come down to earth again.

262 – SKULL CROSSROADS LIGHTNING

General Situation: If you are considering sharing accommodation with someone, or maybe taking a lodger or students into your home, then think this step through very carefully indeed. Your peaceful day-to-day routine could be thrown into chaos and there's nothing like an outsider in the house to build up disagreements and disputes.

Finance/Business: Now is the time to check that all your insurance premiums have been paid up to date (it's quite easy to overlook such matters) and to ensure that your property and possessions are adequately covered for any contingency. Pay special note to the risk of fire and storm damage.

Love/Affection: If your partner seems to be spending a lot more time in front of the mirror lately and spending considerably more time over dress and appearance, don't immediately suspect them of having someone else. They are only doing it to please you at best and at worst they are starting to feel their age or trying to get out of a rut. Relax and stop worrying.

261 – SKULL CROSSROADS SNAIL

General Situation: Life is about to throw you in at the deep end with a whole series of changes which you had not bargained for. Don't worry – you'll be able to cope perfectly well as long as you watch what you're doing and don't allow anyone else to interfere.

Finance/Business: Financially your watchword over the coming months should be 'thrift'. Try to put some money away which will give you security and don't make any major purchases unless it is really necessary.

Love/Affection: A very persuasive stranger may try to steal your affections and this could cause no end of trouble if you allow them to turn your head. Look very carefully before you leap and consider the consequences!

256 – SKULL CAT FRUIT-TREE

General Situation: A long-standing health problem will soon be resolved, perhaps by some new form of treatment but more probably by seeking some form of alternative medicine which could prove costly but effective. Don't begrudge the cost – your health is important.

Finance/Business: Your property represents a very large capital asset as well as a home for you and your family. It needs looking after and now would be a good time to undertake repairs or improvements which are necessary.

Love/Affection: You and your partner could suddenly find yourselves going up in the world with more money to spend on yourselves and your surroundings. This could result from a win of some kind (pools, lottery), but probably from an inheritance.

255 – SKULL CAT GOBLET

General Situation: A wedding in the family could come as quite a surprise. Whoever it is, this announcement will bring some changes to your own life and something which you previously thought impossible can now be achieved.

Finance/Business: A family celebration (wedding/reunion) could see you dipping a little deeper into your pocket than you had anticipated. However, don't go getting yourself into debt over it and try to enjoy yourself – after all, you're paying for it.

Love/Affection: If you are still single then all that could be changing rapidly for you. If, however, you are already married then watch out for very pleasant and totally unexpected changes in your relationship. A good time for all, whatever their marital status.

254 – SKULL CAT KEY

General Situation: A new phase in your life is about to begin very soon which will affect not only you but your family as well. Old problems will be resolved and you will be able to start afresh with few personal worries to hold you back.

Finance/Business: Unexpected financial help from a distant relative couldn't come at a better time. This should enable you not only to pay off any outstanding debts but also to enter into a new venture.

Love/Affection: You and your partner will be offered the chance to try something you have always dreamed of. It's the tonic your relationship has been needing and will alter the views and feelings of you both quite dramatically.

253 – SKULL CAT LADDER

General Situation: A personal ambition may have to be postponed or put aside altogether because of a frustrating health problem or the conflicting plans of a relative. Don't brood about it too much, as you will get another chance and sooner than you think.

Finance/Business: Before dismissing an unexpected opportunity out of hand, just take a little time to think it over first. You could do it if you were sufficiently determined and it would certainly give you a boost. The choice is yours.

Love/Affection: If your partner seems indecisive about something out of the ordinary you might have suggested, make sure that they have completely come round to your way of thinking before you take any positive steps. You could fail without their backing.

252 – SKULL CAT LIGHTNING

General Situation: Any changes in your home or family life which you are planning to make shouldn't be embarked upon until you have given the idea a great deal of consideration. If you don't look at it from everyone's point of view you could make somebody very resentful and irritated.

Finance/Business: Don't take risks, however good the odds may seem at the time. You could lose everything you have worked so hard for, just because you acted impulsively and without care.

Love/Affection: Should your partner decide to turn down an opportunity which, on the face of it, looks very good, don't lose your temper. Once you know all the facts you'll be more understanding.

251 – SKULL CAT SNAIL

General Situation: Should you suddenly decide to throw yourself into a vigorous keep-fit campaign, don't be surprised if you pull a muscle or do some permanent damage. Take things gently.

Finance/Business: Avoid the temptation to make any impulsive buys. If you bother to ask around there's probably someone in your family who has just the thing you want and would be only too glad to give it to you.

Love/Affection: Avoid making waves in your private life. Your partner may not appreciate making changes if you haven't really thought things over first. Play safe.

246 – SKULL KNIFE FRUIT-TREE

General Situation: Now is the time to stop drifting. Get yourself a positive goal to work towards and really make an effort.

Finance/Business: Money worries and mounting bills may have been putting you under considerable strain lately but don't despair, there are changes coming soon which will solve all this. Keep your eyes open and pay special attention to the 'Situations Vacant' page of your local or trade newspaper.

Love/Affection: Someone with money to burn will try to turn your partner's head with expensive gifts and presents. Resist the urge to go looking for trouble, this will only make matters worse. Play it cool – it will die a natural death very soon when the money runs out.

245 – SKULL KNIFE GOBLET

General Situation: Don't allow old family feuds to spoil a get-together which is coming soon, especially if this is a wedding. Instead, why not forget the past, you can all afford to relax then and enjoy yourselves without the constant threat of arguments.

Finance/Business: Money really isn't everything. If you feel tempted to dabble in some dubious deals in order to make extra money, stop and ask yourself if it is really worth the risk. Do you really want that kind of worry hanging over you?

Love/Affection: If a silly quarrel with your partner over money is allowed to get out of hand then you really could have problems. Do everything you can to put matters right. If you have any little confessions to make, then make them now before the whole affair gets out of hand.

244 – SKULL KNIFE KEY

General Situation: It might be a good idea to break away from your present circle of friends and seek new company and interests elsewhere. These people are not very loyal and would leave you in the lurch only too readily, should you no longer be of use to them.

Finance/Business: Don't get involved in any get-rich-quick schemes, however good they sound. There's usually a catch somewhere.

Love/Affection: Try not to let jealousy spoil your relationship as undoubtedly it will if you continually try to catch your partner out. You must make the effort and try to be more trusting in future.

243 – SKULL KNIFE LADDER

General Situation: When embarking on any new projects, first make sure that you really do understand what you are doing and how everything works, especially if this involves using machinery with which you are not familiar. If you remember to put safety first you won't go far wrong.

Finance/Business: Entering into a partnership with a friend might not be such a good idea as it seems. It is better to retain control yourself even if this does mean stretching your finances to the limit.

Love/Affection: You two really must sort out your problems if your relationship is to last. Quarrelling and arguments are not doing either of you any good. Try to communicate more and make any changes, however drastic, that will improve the situation.

242 – SKULL KNIFE LIGHTNING

General Situation: You will have to move fast and do some even faster talking to get yourself out of a mess you could find yourself in. Unfortunately, it's likely to be your own fault. However, it's not too late to reform.

Finance/Business: When faced at work with something unexpected, and not really to your liking, don't over-react and refuse point blank to tackle the problem. A foolish argument now could lead to serious difficulties.

Love/Affection: Your private life is in for a few storms. You are both going to have to iron out one or two problems which cause arguments and if a compromise isn't possible then you could find yourselves going your own separate ways.

241 – SKULL KNIFE SNAIL

General Situation: If the worries and problems of everyday life are really beginning to get you down, then do something about it now before your health starts to deteriorate. Get away for a few days, maybe to friends or relatives, where you can relax. A change and a rest will do you good.

Finance/Business: You should shop around if you intend to purchase an expensive item such as a motor car, stereo unit, video, etc. This way you will not only be able to see all the models available but get the best price too.

Love/Affection: If your personal affairs are in a bit of a turmoil, try not to do anything on the spur of the moment. This could only make matters worse. Don't discuss your problems with anyone – especially not a close friend.

236 – SKULL HEART FRUIT-TREE

General Situation: Life for you is going to change for the better – quite unexpectedly and sooner than you think. Be prepared for a new job, a change in residence, more money, new friends or a new love in your life. The change could be just one or more of these.

Finance/Business: You seem to be possessed of the Midas touch at the moment. Not only do you attract money but you have the necessary knowledge, experience and intuition to use it wisely and make it work for you. This ability could lead to new and exciting job prospects.

Love/Affection: A new and important person will enter your life and friendship will blossom into something deeper. Just one word of warning – is it you they really admire or all the things you have like money, possessions, influence?

235 – SKULL HEART GOBLET

General Situation: A chance is coming for you to do something you have always dreamed about. This opportunity will be closely connected with an old family friend and will have far-reaching consequences.

Finance/Business: Try not to overspend on frivolous pleasures or you could find that, when you are most in need of some money, there is none left.

Love/Affection: Your private life is not going to be quite so private during the next few weeks and you and your partner will be spending a lot of time in the company of others. This will be a busy time for you both.

234 – SKULL HEART KEY

General Situation: Don't let a sudden change in your life catch you out. Instead, make it work for you and turn the situation into a personal triumph. You will surprise both yourself and your friends by the way you handle the matter.

Finance/Business: If offered a new job some distance from home, perhaps even in another country, think very carefully before reaching a decision. You must weigh the pros and cons – the income may well be higher than your present salary but are you prepared to leave your loved ones in order to enjoy it?

Love/Affection: Cheer up – as one door closes another one opens, and that is just what's going to happen for you. Forget the past and instead look forward to the future. You will soon be finding someone new to share it with.

233 – SKULL HEART LADDER

General Situation: It's no good struggling and trying to do everything on your own. Get your family and friends organized – they'll be only too pleased to lend a hand.

Finance/Business: An outstanding insurance claim or legal wrangle will soon be settled. Invest any money you gain with care.

Love/Affection: You and your partner will find yourselves faced with a decision to make which could either prove to be the best move you've ever made or an absolute disaster.

232 – SKULL HEART LIGHTNING

General Situation: A sudden burst of energy will see you rushing about trying to change everything around you. Make sure that it's only your own life you try to organize. If you meddle with other people's plans you could have problems.

Finance/Business: If faced with something new, consult an expert for advice. Maybe one of your friends is qualified in that particular field – ask. Don't attempt to do anything until you have been properly briefed.

Love/Affection: If you tend to have a roving eye – beware! It could spark off trouble.

231 – SKULL HEART SNAIL

General Situation: Allow yourself more time to relax and keep yourself in good shape. Why not take up some new hobby or interest?

Finance/Business: Avoid making financial decisions at the present time, especially if they are in any way involved with family or friends. Very soon you might need every penny you have and it could be embarrassing if you have to call in loans.

Love/Affection: This should be a quiet and peaceful time for you and your partner. You can both afford to take things easy and relax. Avoid making any decisions, whether major or minor ones. Let them wait until you feel refreshed and ready to deal with them.

226 – SKULL STORK FRUIT-TREE

General Situation: Prepare for some major changes in your life over the next few months. These will be beneficial. They will force you out of your rut and make you start to think for yourself again.

Finance/Business: As far as your career is concerned, the field will be clear for you to surge ahead and promote your own ideas. It could result from the resignation of your greatest rival. Make this opportunity work for you.

Love/Affection: A sudden surge of creative energy will come as quite a surprise to your partner. Instead of wondering when you are going to get around to all the jobs that need doing, they'll be telling you to take it easy and take a break instead.

225 – SKULL STORK GOBLET

General Situation: A good time to tidy up all those odd jobs which you never get around to. Once they're all out of the way you'll be able to devote your time to more relaxing pursuits.

Finance/Business: An error made by a colleague will be to your advantage but resist the temptation to crow over it. Use your own ingenuity and know-how to put matters right.

Love/Affection: Make yourself clearly understood if you are planning something special with your partner. Decide who is to do what if you want your plans to go without a hitch.

224 – SKULL STORK KEY

General Situation: You might be forced to do some rethinking about the course your life is taking. Opportunities are there for you, provided you have sufficient drive and ambition to cope with them.

Finance/Business: Chances for investment might soon arise but beware of schemes with low rates of return. Don't invest more than you can afford to lose.

Love/Affection: There is an offer coming your way which will certainly be worth considering. It could well be the answer to your prayers and it might also solve a lot of problems too.

223 – SKULL STORK LADDER

General Situation: It's time for a good shake-up of anything and everything. Think up a few new ideas or brighten up your old ones. Find something fresh to aim for.

Finance/Business: There could possibly be some confusion over an idea which is primarily yours. Make sure that everyone knows it. Speak up for yourself as there are others only too ready to take the credit.

Love/Affection: You must not allow your partner to manipulate you when faced with a decision you have to make.

222 – SKULL STORK LIGHTNING

General Situation: You will probably have to make a snap decision over something and it could have far-reaching consequences. You may be criticized for your actions but you will be proved right in the long run.

Finance/Business: An unexpected change in your financial affairs will benefit not only you but your immediate family. Take the trouble to explain the situation to them carefully.

Love/Affection: Someone new who will suddenly enter your life could, at first appearances, look to be the one you have been waiting for. Don't do anything hasty – you may have been mistaken.

221 – SKULL STORK SNAIL

General Situation: Try to plan your life so that you have some spare time for relaxation. It's all very well taking on every new opportunity as they arise so long as you are fit enough to cope with it all.

Finance/Business: In order to take on a new financial commitment it will be necessary to take stock of your overall position. See what you really have got, what you could possibly do without and where you can make economies.

Love/Affection: In order to regain your partner's respect and admiration you must try to stand on your own two feet a little more. Try not to be so demanding and become more independent. Not only will it make you more attractive to your partner but it will give you more confidence too.

216 – SKULL SUN FRUIT-TREE

General Situation: If you are feeling happy now, then something new and exciting which could happen soon should leave you feeling positively elated. You will be able to surge ahead and achieve some of the goals you have been aiming for.

Finance/Business: The emphasis for you at the moment is on hard work but not without big rewards at the end of it. Don't allow the odd unexpected surprise or two to take you aback, keep your target in mind and work steadily towards it.

Love/Affection: This is a good time to go into partnership. If you are single then marriage would seem to be indicated – if already married then a joint venture of some kind would be appropriate.

215 – SKULL SUN GOBLET

General Situation: A health problem of long-standing could be much improved by some new form of treatment, bringing with it a new lease of life, more drive and more energy. This is a time when you should enjoy yourself, visit friends or maybe try something different that has not previously been possible.

Finance/Business: Put past mistakes behind you and make the most of what you have. A complete reorganization of your working life is needed. Use your energies to really push for what you want even if it seems that you are reaching too high. You will probably succeed and have cause for celebration. Force the issue by taking the initiative.

Love/Affection: Changes within the family are likely reasons for you to celebrate – maybe a family wedding or christening. If your partner is feeling a little down or undemonstrative, it's up to you to take the lead and cheer him/her up.

214 – SKULL SUN KEY

General Situation: Forget about the past. The future is more important so stop thinking about what might have been. Seize every opportunity that comes your way and work towards something positive and rewarding instead.

Finance/Business: Just because things you have tried to do in the past have failed that's no reason to believe that any new ventures are automatically doomed to failure. Set about solving problems you may have and don't turn down new opportunities on the strength of past misfortunes.

Love/Affection: A few sudden changes will alter the situation between you and your partner and what you make of the situation is entirely up to you. Maybe your children will leave home giving you more time alone together, or a change of residence or occupation could bring about alterations in your lifestyle.

213 – SKULL SUN LADDER

General Situation: If you really want to fulfil a secret ambition then you must take a calm and objective view of everything. Don't allow emotion or a personal bias to cloud the issue as you will only be fooling yourself. An unexpected windfall will also help.

Finance/Business: You could find yourself faced with one or two unforseen expenses which were totally unbudgeted for. Try not to let this dampen your enthusiasm or throw you off course in any way.

Love/Affection: It's about time you two buried the hatched and if you really can't agree about something then find a working compromise instead. Life is too short to be continually arguing so forget your pride and make the first move.

212 – SKULL SUN LIGHTNING

General Situation: Try not to let your mind wander, especially if you are doing something which is potentially dangerous like driving or using an electrically-driven appliance. Accidents happen quickly and most can easily be avoided if a little care is taken.

Finance/Business: Make sure that all your personal possessions or business assets are adequately insured, especially against fire or storm damage. Also make sure that if you have business premises all the safety rules and regulations have been adhered to. A little time spent now could represent money saved later.

Love/Affection: A little unexpected opposition may not be a bad thing as far as your private life is concerned. A good shake-up could be what you need to make you realize just how lucky you are and how much your partner means to you.

211 – SKULL SUN SNAIL

General Situation: An old health problem could flare up again and may well slow you down for a while. Try not to get too despondent if there are things you desperately want to get on with and resist the urge to bore other people with your troubles.

Finance/Business: Not a good time to make any financial moves whether buying or selling. If you do, you could come unstuck as some fairly drastic changes in your economic climate are coming. Far better to watch and wait for the time being.

Love/Affection: If you really want your relationship to survive then you must handle it with great care. Try not to be so dominant and aggressive – show a little more love and consideration and your partner will not fail to respond favourably.

166 – WEB CROSSROADS FRUIT-TREE

General Situation: You may find that new acquaintances you have met are not quite as pleasant as they would have you believe. They may only want to be friendly in order to use you in some way.

Finance/Business: If you have the opportunity to buy something on the cheap, especially a domestic appliance such as a television or washing machine, make sure that everything is above board.

Love/Affection: There's nothing quite like money to spark off rows between husband and wife. If you have spent rather more than you had intended on a hobby or a personal luxury you would be well advised to confess before some interfering neighbour or acquaintance says something precipitous.

165 – WEB CROSSROADS GOBLET

General Situation: At a party or social gathering of some kind you will meet a great many new and intriguing people. However, before you decide to become too involved with any of them, find out just a little bit more about their backgrounds.

Finance/Business: Don't allow the lavish hospitality at a business conference or trade show affect your judgement in any way. These people are only trying to promote themselves and are not really interested in you as a person.

Love/Affection: You could become involved with someone new who you meet at a party or through friends. By all means enjoy their company but be very suspicious if they ask you to do them a big favour almost immediately.

164 – WEB CROSSROADS KEY

General Situation: When opportunity comes knocking at your door make sure you know exactly what risks are involved before you decide to open it. Once you are involved it will be very difficult to back out later.

Finance/Business: If you have any financial difficulties and problems then you must try to solve them by yourself. Once you call in the assistance of other people, especially professionals, you could be letting yourself in for all sorts of unforseen expenses.

Love/Affection: If you and your partner are going through a rough patch at the moment, don't give up. Work together to put matters right. Whatever you do, avoid pouring your heart out to a complete stranger, however sympathetic they may seem, it could make matters worse.

163 – WEB CROSSROADS LADDER

General Situation: If you want to better yourself and really get on, then take the trouble to look at others and find out how they have managed it. Talk to them and learn from their mistakes.

Finance/Business: Try not to get too caught up in other people's enthusiasm. Something which may be very easy and profitable for them may not be half so easy for you and could be a financial disaster too. Watch and admire if you must but don't get involved yourself.

Love/Affection: If you are being deceptive and underhand you can be sure that your partner will find you out – one way or another. There's always someone only too ready to pass on a bit of gossip.

162 – WEB CROSSROADS LIGHTNING

General Situation: Life is full of surprises and a foreigner, who you will shortly meet, could have one or two for you – especially if you ask them into your home and introduce them to your family.

Finance/Business: Don't be in too much of a rush to get involved in a business deal which has overseas connections. Acquaint yourself with all the rules and regulations concerning foreign business.

Love/Affection: Whatever you do, don't allow yourself to become involved in the domestic arguments of a neighbour or friend. Lending a sympathetic ear is one thing, but proffering advice could land you in trouble.

161 – WEB CROSSROADS SNAIL

General Situation: If you have reached the point when you feel you could do with a break and get away from everything for a few days, think carefully before you decide where to go. Don't just turn up unannounced on friends, however well you know them or you could arrive in the middle of a domestic crisis.

Finance/Business: Think very carefully before you decide to lend anyone money. It could well be the last you see of it. Far wiser to say no and risk offence than to say yes and be the loser.

Love/Affection: Should you hear some gossip concerning your partner, don't allow it to colour your feelings for them. Confront them openly with what you have heard and hear their side of the story.

156 – WEB CAT FRUIT-TREE

General Situation: Most families have a black sheep – and should he or she turn up unannounced, make sure that everything is kept on a very friendly footing and that old feuds and grievances, especially about money, are kept well out of the conversation.

Finance/Business: If you are involved with family trust funds or wills, especially if you are named as executor, make sure that everything is properly organized.

Love/Affection: If you and your partner have recently come into some money, make sure that he/she gets their fair share or you could find yourself unjustly accused of trickery. Don't fall out over money.

155 – WEB CAT GOBLET

General Situation: Avoid turning down an invitation to a family gathering because you don't think you'll enjoy it. Go along, enter into the spirit of things and you'll be surprised how much you'll benefit.

Finance/Business: If you are expected to pay a large bill for something like a wedding, try to keep costs down as much as possible. There is a chance you could waste a great deal.

Love/Affection: If you and your family do not always see eye to eye about your choice of partner, don't allow them to involve you in a public argument over the subject. This applies especially if you will shortly be attending a social function at which other members of your family will be present.

154 – WEB CAT KEY

General Situation: If you can see that a member of your family is about to get involved in something rather risky then give them the benefit of your experience and point out the pitfalls to them. They may choose to totally ignore your wisdom but, at least, you will know that you did try to warn them.

Finance/Business: If you have any financial worries that you find difficult to cope with, it might be a good idea to talk things over with your family to see what they can come up with. You might be able to unravel the problem between you.

Love/Affection: If you are looking for a way to wriggle out of an entanglement which is becoming more and more involved, seek advice from a relative who has been in a similar situation and may be able to help. Once you have decided how to handle matters, wait for the right moment to act.

153 – WEB CAT LADDER

General Situation: Try not to let your family interfere in your personal ambitions however well-meaning they may be. Listen to the advice they offer, it could well be good, but in the long run you must decide what's going to be done and how you want to do it.

Finance/Business: You must think very carefully about all the disadvantages before you decide to run a business from home. You may save the time usually spent travelling and economize on outgoings but what about the distractions? – children, pets, callers, household chores. It could be disastrous for your concentration.

Love/Affection: Don't let family squabbles and petty jealousies come between you and your partner. And don't let your family encroach on your spare time!

152 – WEB CAT LIGHTNING

General Situation: If you are involved in something which your family are unaware of and which they would strongly disapprove of, you had better tie up any loose ends without delay if you wish to avoid detection. Or better still – confess the whole affair and clear your conscience.

Finance/Business: Hang on to your money and avoid buying frivolous items.

Love/Affection: Sharing your life with someone is not quite so easy as it seems and if you want it to succeed you will have to give as well as take. So don't be surprised, if you do something inconsiderate once too often, that you find yourself at the centre of a row.

151 – WEB CAT SNAIL

General Situation: Beware of hidden problems. You can only overcome them by approaching all matters with caution at the moment.

Finance/Business: Be careful if you are tempted to invest in an 'antique'. It's very easy to make mistakes.

Love/Affection: Don't allow your partner to draw you into an argument concerning either your family or his/hers. Proceed with care – don't take sides, and change the subject if at all possible.

146 – WEB KNIFE FRUIT-TREE

General Situation: Not a good time for you at the moment. Everything you have worked for seems to be vulnerable and at risk. But try not to get too depressed and don't make any hasty, snap decisions. Don't let your own carelessness involve you in an accident.

Finance/Business: The night of the long knives! Workplace politics, crafty dealings and confusion are rife. Even your job or financial position could be in jeopardy. Avoid any decisions until you know who you can trust, and don't underwrite anyone else's schemes as this could bring problems.

Love/Affection: Possibly someone close to you is up to something a little underhand and, although you can sense something wrong, it will be very hard to identify the problem. All you can do is keep your ears and eyes open and try not to say things you might later regret if drawn into an argument. It is especially important that you do not quarrel over money.

145 – WEB KNIFE GOBLET

General Situation: Definitely not a good time to go filling your diary with social engagements of any kind at all. There may be safety in numbers but right now the greater the number the greater the risk of deception, guile, insincerity and duplicity. Stay at home with a good book.

Finance/Business: There's something slightly underhand going on around you so keep your ears open and see what information you can pick up that might be to your advantage. Don't act on it too quickly.

Love/Affection: Your partner probably has a lot to put up with having you as his/her other half. Relax more and stop seeing problems where none exist.

144 – WEB KNIFE KEY

General Situation: Don't allow plotting and scheming by others around you to spoil your chances. Keep your sights set firmly on your own objectives and do the best you can.

Finance/Business: Industrial disputes could cause you heavy financial losses either directly or indirectly. You must try to find a way to reopen communications between management and unions.

Love/Affection: If your private affairs seem to be in a state of turmoil and you don't really know what to do for the best, then do nothing. Let matters ride for a while longer even if you are really discontented – time has its own way of solving problems if you are only prepared to wait long enough.

143 – WEB KNIFE LADDER

General Situation: Try to maintain a calm exterior even if you are feeling liable to explode at any moment. Losing your temper will only make you appear foolish. Get a firm grip on yourself and deal with your problems one by one.

Finance/Business: Try not to be so easily discouraged and defeatist. Don't be manipulated and downtrodden – you will need all your courage and determination to succeed.

Love/Affection: The presence of a new colleague of the opposite sex will prove to be a great distraction and also something of a temptation. It really depends upon how good a relationship you have with your partner at present as to how you act.

142 – WEB KNIFE LIGHTNING

General Situation: If you are prepared to act quickly then you will soon be able to solve a major problem in your life. Don't expect that this will be an easy course to take because it will not. You'll have to work hard and put all your skills to the test. Are you up to the challenge, and can you put other temptations aside?

Finance/Business: Try to be as independent as you possibly can and don't rely so much on other people to get you out of difficulties. If you consider matters carefully and do not do anything rash you should be able to avoid most financial pitfalls. Be more confident.

Love/Affection: Even though someone you are very fond of seems to be making rather a mess of their lives you must not get involved in their problems if you value that friendship. Any offer of help or advice from you could be totally misunderstood. Be prepared to pick up the pieces if necessary, but don't interfere.

141 – WEB KNIFE SNAIL

General Situation: Do not allow the friction and feuding of those around you to undermine your own health. Their arguments are no concern of yours. Lend a sympathetic ear if you think it might help but don't get trapped into taking sides. You must remain neutral.

Finance/Business: Financially you are best advised to make no moves at all until new guidelines have been established.

Love/Affection: Resist the temptation to involve yourself in matchmaking – however well-suited you may think the two people are. It's a bad idea to manipulate people, however good your intentions may be.

136 – WEB HEART FRUIT-TREE

General Situation: Make sure that, when you are out and about with friends, you're not always the one who has to foot the bill. You work hard for the money you earn so be on the lookout for others only too ready to spend it for you.

Finance/Business: One of your so-called 'friends' at work, who you thought you could trust, is about to show him/herself in their true colours. Their activities will soon be discovered. Don't let yourself be labelled guilty by association.

Love/Affection: Don't try to impress someone special in your life by putting on an act and trying to be something you're not. Far better to be yourself than risk being exposed as a fraud at a later date.

135 – WEB HEART GOBLET

General Situation: Get out of the rat race for a while and try to spend more time with your family and friends. You'll be able to relax in the company of people you trust instead of having to keep on your toes in case someone is after your job or checking up on you to make sure that you are doing it properly.

Finance/Business: If some pet project of yours at work (or a hobby) which has cost you considerable sums of money doesn't seem to be succeeding or as fulfilling as you had hoped – then write it off. Any more you spend on it will be wasted.

Love/Affection: If your emotional encounters have been disappointing recently and you are feeling a bit down and unloved, then why not look up some old friends and find out what they have been up to lately.

134 – WEB HEART KEY

General Situation: If you feel that life is somehow passing you by and that you would like to live a little more, get out and about. The chances are that new interests will bring you the opportunities you are looking for.

Finance/Business: You should try to show a little more care when handling your own affairs. Make sure that you don't get short-changed when out shopping and lending money, to even your closest friend, is inadvisable and could cause problems.

Love/Affection: Honesty is the best policy, whether married or single, if you want to get the best out of a relationship. Avoid being underhand in any way.

133 – WEB HEART LADDER

General Situation: New opportunities are coming your way which could bring great successes. However, try to reach your goal by honest methods or you could lose a few friends on the way.

Finance/Business: If you are thinking of applying for a new job, particularly one where a friend could put in a good word for you, make sure that you have the necessary qualifications. You'll be wasting everyone's time if the position is beyond your capabilities and your friend will be made to look foolish too.

Love/Affection: Put your own hobbies and interests to one side and spend more of your leisure time with your partner. It will improve your relationship and you can always go back to them at a later date.

132 – WEB HEART LIGHTNING

General Situation: Try to avoid doing anything rash at the moment. Your family and friends are sure to misunderstand your motives.

Finance/Business: Should a really good opportunity arise to make some money quickly, don't waste time seeking advice but act fast and let your own feelings be your guide on this occasion.

Love/Affection: If you want to keep your partner's love and trust, then don't go discussing your private affairs with other people. Not everyone can keep confidences to themselves and the last thing you both want are others gossiping about you behind your backs. You should sort out your own problems between you.

131 – WEB HEART SNAIL

General Situation: Someone who you are very fond of is overdoing it and you know it. Try to make them take things easier and help them whenever you can as they seem to have a lot on their plate at present.

Finance/Business: Try to avoid making decisions concerning money if at all possible. Play for time while you check the situation. By using delaying tactics you could spot something going on which you might otherwise not have noticed.

Love/Affection: Show a little more compassion for your partner – he/she may not really be feeling well but is doing his/her best to hide it from you. Go out of your way to lend a hand and make sure that they take it easy until they are fully recovered.

126 – WEB STORK FRUIT-TREE

General Situation: Now is the time to plan improvements for both home and work. Be more creative and imaginative, but resist the temptation to wander off into the realms of fantasy – your schemes must be feasible.

Finance/Business: If your talents and creative abilities are not fully appreciated where you work at present, consider applying for another job or even becoming self-employed. There are some drawbacks to this but if you have half the ability and resourcefulness you think you have, then you'll survive.

Love/Affection: Where your private life is concerned, try to forget about past involvements as they are over and done with – brooding won't help. Instead, try to concentrate on your future and work hard at it. Above all, don't go making the same mistakes all over again, you should have learned your lesson by now.

125 – WEB STORK GOBLET

General Situation: Life for you will soon improve dramatically and you will be involved in the organization of an important project. This could be the chance you have been waiting for to try out new ideas and concepts. Be creative and don't be afraid to experiment.

Finance/Business: Don't be in too much of a hurry to spend all your spare money on a hobby or entertainment but keep a little back for a rainy day. You'll be glad that you did as the opportunity to tackle something new could soon present itself and you will certainly need the money then.

Love/Affection: As far as personal affairs are concerned, this could be a very unsettled and confusing time for you. This period will soon pass.

124 – WEB STORK KEY

General Situation: Your chance to use your imagination and flair for organization is coming and it will certainly get you out of the rut you are in. Important and influential people will become involved in your life and will be of great assistance to you, both now and in the future.

Finance/Business: It is likely that you will be invited to join some form of professional or business partnership very soon. Treat this offer with some caution, especially if you are required to invest your own money in the venture.

Love/Affection: Try not to spend so much of your time worrying about the stability of your relationship with your partner. There is really no need.

123 – WEB STORK LADDER

General Situation: If you dream of advancement, go ahead and try – you are quite capable of achieving success. Handle people with care and consideration – you may need their help one day.

Finance/Business: Before embarking on any new schemes, make sure that they really are viable propositions.

Love/Affection: Find the time to talk to your partner in private and make sure that his/her dreams and aspirations really are the same as yours before getting involved in long-term schemes. You could be surprised at the answers you get.

122 – WEB STORK LIGHTNING

General Situation: Avoid putting too many irons in the fire at once and resist the temptation to take on more than you can comfortably handle. This will only cause confusion and carelessness.

Finance/Business: Don't allow other people to take advantage of your good nature. You will be the one who takes the blame if things go wrong and besides, you really haven't the time to spare. You should have enough work of your own to fully occupy your time.

Love/Affection: If your partner is putting some kind of pressure on you to reach a quick decision over a personal matter, try to delay for as long as possible. This will give you time to think things over.

121 – WEB STORK SNAIL

General Situation: Although you may be feeling at the peak of physical condition you should take care of your health. Any strenuous activities, especially a new sport, should be approached carefully.

Finance/Business: Financially this is a time for taking stock of your resources, thinking and planning but not doing. If you go over your plans for the future carefully and meticulously you should be able to spot potential trouble spots.

Love/Affection: If the stresses and strains of everyday life have been getting you down lately and your plans and ideas have been beset with problems and complications, then talk things over with your partner. The love and concern they show for you will have a stabilizing effect on you.

116 – WEB SUN FRUIT-TREE

General Situation: Try not to get sidetracked if you want to make headway and achieve a personal ambition. There will be plenty of time later to do other things, but right now you must drive yourself on and reach your goal.

Finance/Business: If you want to avoid financial disaster you must learn to live within your means and stop pretending that you are better off than you really are. Take stock of your situation and see where economies can be made.

Love/Affection: Money, success and the power that goes with it can attract the wrong sort of people. Try to play down your achievements and don't make such a show of your possessions.

115 – WEB SUN GOBLET

General Situation: Don't fall into the old trap of saying more than you mean when relaxed and off your guard. Alcohol not only loosens your tongue but it also impairs your judgement – avoid discussing your private affairs over a round of drinks.

Finance/Business: Your drive and ambitious nature could be responsible for your promotion at work. However, try not to count your chickens too soon.

Love/Affection: If you are not careful you could find yourself, through no fault of your own, in a very complicated situation involving a divorcee you will meet at a party or social gathering. Handle this delicate problem with kid gloves or you could stir up all sorts of trouble for both yourself and your family.

114 – WEB SUN KEY

General Situation: You seem to have a natural talent for helping others to overcome their problems and difficulties. However, you must remember that when you become involved in other people's affairs you may sometimes become privvy to confidential information. Don't repeat what you hear.

Finance/Business: You already have the key to your financial success although you may not have known how to use it before. You can listen and you can speak and that's just what you must do. Listen to other people who have done well for themselves and hear how they did it.

Love/Affection: You can't go on playing the field for ever and although you may have narrowed it down to two runners, you still have to make a choice soon or you could end up with no-one. Choose the one who makes you happy.

113 – WEB SUN LADDER

General Situation: Honesty is always the best policy so don't be tempted to say you can do something when you know in your heart that it's beyond you. You are sure to get caught out at some point and could ruin your chances for the future.

Finance/Business: Now is the time to 'pull your socks up' before it's too late and double your efforts. The choice is yours.

Love/Affection: You and your partner will soon find yourselves working together very hard on something which you both share a passion for – this could well be renovating an old house. You are both extremely determined people when you set your minds on something and are sure to succeed. Watch out, however, for minor snags and pitfalls which could slow your progress.

112 – WEB SUN LIGHTNING

General Situation: You will have to act quickly if you want to make the most of an opportunity you will soon be offered. Rapid and accurate calculations will also be called for as you won't have time to recheck anything later on.

Finance/Business: Don't sign or commit yourself to anything unless you are properly in the picture and have had everything explained to you.

Love/Affection: Try not to be quite so self-centred for a change, your career won't fall into ruins if you take a night off and relax with your partner. Don't be quite so serious all the time.

111 – WEB SUN SNAIL

General Situation: Plan to spend an entire day doing nothing except enjoying yourself or have a lazy time with friends. All those important, complicated tasks which you ought to be getting on with will still be there but today you should unwind and take it easy.

Finance/Business: Try to keep your financial dealings as simple and as uncomplicated as possible if you want to avoid unnecessary worry and stress. The more complex you allow your dealings to become the more you increase the risk of confusion and trouble. Practise simplicity for peace of mind.

Love/Affection: If there are subjects not for discussion in your relationship, which you know are potential trouble spots, such as money, religion, relatives and so on, then steer clear of them if you want to avoid complications. Collect your thoughts before you speak and that way your relationship should stay happy and successful.

BIBLIOGRAPHY

ADDIS, W. E. & ARNOLD, Thomas *A Catholic Dictionary* (Virtue & Co. Ltd. London).

BROWN, Raymond Lamont *A Book of Superstitions* (David & Charles 1970).

CIRLOT, J. E. *A Dictionary of Symbols* (Routledge & Kegan Paul Ltd. 1962).

COOPER, J. C. *An Illustrated Encyclopedia of Traditional Symbols.*

HILL, Douglas *Magic & Superstition* (Hamlyn, London 1968).

JONES, Gertrude *Dictionary of Mythology Folklore & Symbols.*

LAMB, Geoffrey *Magic Charms & Talismans.*

SMITH, Christine *The Book of Divination.*

VILLIERS, Elizabeth *The Book of Charms* (Lorrimer Publishing Ltd. London, 1973).

Encyclopaedia Britannica (Volume 5).

Oxford Junior Encyclopaedia.

Everyman's Encyclopaedia.

The Interpreters Dictionary of the Bible (Abingdon Press, N.Y.)

A Guide to Greek & Roman Life (London 1929).

INDEX

Adam (and Eve), 47
Agamemnon, 16
Astragli, 11, 12, 16

Backgammon, 15
Beetle, 21
Bettinis, 54
Boat, 25
Bones, 11
Book of the Dead, 53
Boot, 25
Buddhists, 55

Cardano, Gerolamo, 14
Cat, 35
Chalice, 49, 50
Chambers, 40
'Chance Bone', 16
Chaucer, Geoffrey, 41
Chelmsford Witches, 36
Claddagh Rings, 40
Conway, 36
Crossroads, 33
Crown and Anchor, 16
Cup, 49

Day of Judgement, 40
Diana, 50
Dollar Sign, 47

Easter, 38

'Five-Stones', 16
Fleur-de-Lis, 39
Fruit Tree, 47

Galileo, 14
Goblet, 49

Hamlet, 28
Hanged Man, 16
Hazard, 16
Heart, 39
Hecate, 35, 51
Hindus, 56
Holy Grail, 49
Horseshoe, 22
Horus, 53
Huygens, Christiaan, 14

I Ching, 11

Indra, 56
Isis, 22

Jacob, 54
Jana, 50
Janus, 51
Jung, C. G., 20
Jupiter, 56

Key, 50
Key of Life, 50
Knife, 36

Ladder, 52
Leblant, 28
Leo, 43, 65
Lightning, 53
Lots, 11, 12
Lotus Flower, 40
Luckenbooths, 39
Lug, 58

Mahabharata, 13
Mare, 52
Mercury, 12, 50
Muspelheim, 43

Nelson, 24
Nem Ankh, 51

Orpheus, 28

Palamedes, 13
Plato, 28
Pound Sign, 47, 48

Ra, 43
Rgveda, 13
Romanies, 52
Rose, 40

Scarab, 21
Scott, W., 31
Senet, 16
Shiva, 56
Skull, 28
Snail, 57
Solar Boat, 27
Sophocles, 13
Stork, 41
Sun, 43, 44
Swastika, 50

Talaria, 12
Tarot, 15, 44, 50, 56
Threshold of Life, 51
Throwsticks, 11
Tower Struck by Lightning, The, 56
Trinity (Holy), 17, 20

Venus, 41
Venus, Throw of, 16

Web, 30

Ymir, 28